Edition KWV

Die „Edition KWV" beinhaltet hochwertige Werke aus dem Bereich der Wirtschaftswissen-schaften. Alle Werke in der Reihe erschienen ursprünglich im Kölner Wissenschaftsverlag, dessen Programm Springer Gabler 2018 übernommen hat.

Weitere Bände in der Reihe http://www.springer.com/series/16033

Florian Defregger

Revenue Management for Manufacturing Companies

 Springer Gabler

Florian Defregger
Wiesbaden, Germany

Bis 2018 erschien der Titel im Kölner Wissenschaftsverlag, Köln
Dissertation Katholische Universität Eichstätt-Ingolstadt, 2009

Edition KWV
ISBN 978-3-658-24036-3   ISBN 978-3-658-24037-0   (eBook)
https://doi.org/10.1007/978-3-658-24037-0

Library of Congress Control Number: 2018968336

Springer Gabler
© Springer Fachmedien Wiesbaden GmbH, part of Springer Nature 2009, Reprint 2019
Originally published by Kölner Wissenschaftsverlag, Köln, 2009

This Springer Gabler imprint is published by the registered company Springer Fachmedien Wiesbaden GmbH part of Springer Nature
The registered company address is: Abraham-Lincoln-Str. 46, 65189 Wiesbaden, Germany

Preface

This dissertation is the result of my research work at the Chair of Production Management at the Faculty of Business Administration and Economics of the Catholic University of Eichstätt-Ingolstadt in the years 2001 to 2006. After his yearly production research meeting in Greece, my doctoral thesis supervisor, Prof. Dr. Heinrich Kuhn, suggested to take a look at a proceedings article of Kniker and Burman (2001). This article dealt with applying an operations research technique called revenue management, which was mainly used in the service sector up to this point, to the manufacturing sector.

After delving into the article I figured out that I now had a stochastic operations research topic although I had tried to avoid stochastics as much as possible during my previous studies. My knowledge accumulated for my diploma thesis on deterministic lotsizing on parallel machines certainly was of very little value for this topic. Nonetheless, after getting the book of Puterman (1994) and exploring the world of stochastic decision processes, I got to know and appreciate this world, while in parallel I was fittingly assigned to deepen students' knowledge of stochastic models in production systems.

After many intellectual sweats and tears I managed to finish my dissertation by September 2006. For the oral tests, though, the doctoral examination regulations dictate presenting two rather small theses which are not supposed to have any relation to the dissertation topic. After coming up with the first hypothesis concerned with opposing numerical student ratings of teachers, the second topic took quite some time because the first choice of topic did not prove really fruitful. After settling for a second choice of opposing national minimum wages, the oral tests took place successfully in January 2009.

I want to thank Prof. Dr. Heinrich Kuhn for providing me with an interesting research topic which also resulted in several joint publications. I also want to thank my second thesis supervisor, Prof. Dr. Ulrich Küsters, to make the effort of reading through and refereeing my dissertation. Furthermore, I want to thank my colleagues at the Chair of Production Management, Dr. Daniel Quadt and Dr. Georg Krieg for providing me with many interesting discussions which most of the time did not have much to do with my research topic but were interesting nonetheless.

Also, I want to thank my wife Serene for providing me with continuous love and support and my parents for enabling me the education that was a prerequisite for this dissertation. Lastly, I want to thank God for empowering me to finish this project.

Freiburg im Breisgau, June 2009 Florian Defregger

Contents

List of Figures

List of Tables

List of Symbols

Estimates are denoted by a hat, e.g. $\hat{g}$ is an estimate of g.

A	number of artificial order classes
a	an artificial order class
C_s	confidence interval for the sth proportion
c	remaining number of periods the capacity is booked out
$c^{\max}$	maximum that c can reach
$D(i)$	set of decisions that can be taken in state i
$|D|$	maximum number of decisions that can be taken in a certain state
d	a decision
$F(x)$	distribution function of supposedly lower values to be tested with the Mann-Whitney test
$G(x)$	distribution function of supposedly higher values to be tested with the Mann-Whitney test
g	average reward per period
$g(I)$	average reward resulting from a FCFS policy using a maximum inventory level of I
$g(\pi)$	average reward resulting from policy π
$g(\omega)$	average reward resulting from a policy that rejects ω artificial order classes
H_0	null hypothesis
H_1	alternative hypothesis
h	unit inventory holding cost per period
$\underline{h}, \overline{h}$	lower, upper bound for h

$\tilde{I}$ maximum inventory level

$\underline{I}, \overline{I}$ lower, upper bound for $\tilde{I}$

I_1, I_2 maximum inventory levels to be compared

I^{max} maximum inventory capacity

i current level of inventory

$\tilde{i}$ inventory threshold

l^{max} maximum lead time, given by $l^{\mathrm{max}} = \max_n l_n$

l_n lead time for an order of class n

$\underline{l}_n$ lower bound for the lead time for an order of class n

m_n profit margin for an order of class n

m_n^{rel} relative profit margin for an order of class n

N number of order classes

n an order class

O variable to denote wether a company has the potential for revenue management

o_{mn} setup cost from order class m to order class n

o_{mn}^{rel} relative setup cost from order class m to order class n

$P^d(i,j)$ transition probability from state i to state j if decision d is taken

$P^\pi(i,j)$ transition probability from state i to state j under policy π

$\tilde{P}^d(i)$ stationary probability of state i if decision d is taken

$\tilde{P}^\pi(i)$ stationary probability of state i under policy π

p_n arrival probability for an order of class n in each period

$R^d(i)$ reward that is received when decision d is taken in state i

$R^\pi(i)$ reward that is received when the system enters state i under policy π

r share of u_n in x_n

S set of all states

$|S|$ number of all states

$|S|^{\mathrm{real}}$ actual number of states for a problem instance

$S_d(i)$ number of source states of state i where decision d is taken

S_d^{max} maximum number of source states where decision d is taken

S^{max}	maximum number of source states where any decision is taken
$S_{v=0}$	set of states with a relative value of 0
s	current setup state
t_{mn}	setup time from order class m to order class n
$\bar{t}_n$	average of the setup times $t_{mn}, \forall m$ into order class n
$\bar{t}'_n$	average of the setup times $t_{mn}, m \neq n$ into order class n
U	size of a company
u_n	capacity usage in periods for an order of class n
$V_n(i)$	value of state i if the stochastic process would end in n periods
$v(i)$	relative value of state i
W	variable to denote wether a company uses revenue management
$X_{\pi i}$	average reward obtained from replication i under policy π
X_{1i}, X_{2i}	average rewards obtained from replication i under two policies that are currently compared
$\overline{X}_\pi(n)$	average of the average rewards $X_{\pi i}$ after n replications
x_n	sum of u_n and $\bar{t}_n$
x'_n	sum of u_n and $\bar{t}'_n$
Z_i	difference of two average rewards X_{1i} and X_{2i}
$\overline{Z}(n)$	average of the Z_i after n replications
α	level of significance
α_s	level of significance for the sth proportion
β	special convergence criterion for the Gauss-Seidel iterative method
γ	maximum relative error of simulation estimates $\overline{X}_\pi(n)$
$\Delta^{\mathrm{FCFS-opt}}$	percentage deviation of the average reward of a FCFS policy compared to the optimal average reward
$\Delta^{\mathrm{H-opt}}$	percentage deviation of the average reward of a heuristic policy compared to the optimal average reward
$\Delta V(i)$	difference of $V_n(i)$ and $V_{n-1}(i)$, given by $\Delta V(i) = V_n(i) - V_{n-1}(i)$
$\underline{\Delta V}$	lower bound for all $\Delta V(i)$

$\overline{\Delta V}$	upper bound for all $\Delta V(i)$
δ	convergence criterion for the Gauss-Seidel iterative method
ϵ	convergence criterion for the value iteration method
θ^T	vector of τ_n, $\theta^T = (\tau_0, \tau_1, \ldots, \tau_N)$
ι	number of units taken from the inventory to fulfill an order
$\iota_{\min}$	minimum amount of inventory that has to be used in order to fulfill an accepted order
$\iota_{\max}$	maximum amount of inventory that can be used in order to fulfill an accepted order
μ_s	true value of the sth proportion
$\tilde{\omega}$	best number of rejected artificial order classes found by the heuristic procedure
$\underline{\omega}, \overline{\omega}$	lower, upper bound for $\tilde{\omega}$
ω_1, ω_2	numbers of rejected artificial order classes to be compared
Π	investigation period
π	a policy for a Markov decision process
π^{com}	policy which induces an irreducible Markov reward process
π^{FCFS}	FCFS policy
π^{opt}	optimal policy for a Markov decision process
π^ϵ	average reward of the ϵ-optimal policy
$\tilde{\pi}$	best policy found by a heuristic procedure
$\tilde{\pi}^{\text{opt}}$	approximate optimal policy found by the value iteration algorithm
ρ	traffic intensity
$\tilde{\rho}$	approximate traffic intensity
ρ_n	traffic intensity of order class n
σ_n	share of order class n in the traffic intensity ρ
$\underline{\sigma}, \overline{\sigma}$	global lower, upper bound for all σ_n
$\overline{\sigma}_v$	variable upper bound for σ_n
τ_n	heuristic order acceptance threshold of order class n

Chapter 1

Introduction

1.1 Motivation and Outline

In a global competitive market, companies are always trying to improve their profitability. A tool which has proven successful in order to achieve this goal with relatively low technological investments has been the use of revenue management systems. However, these systems have only been implemented in service industries, see Talluri and van Ryzin (2004). Thus, the question arises if revenue management could be profitably applied for manufacturing companies, as well.

This dissertation tries to answer this question. For this purpose, the remainder of this chapter describes the field of revenue management and concludes with a thorough literature review regarding theoretical models concerning the application of revenue management in a manufacturing context.

In the second chapter, an empirical study is described which answers two important research questions with regards to revenue management for manufacturing companies. Do some companies already implicitly use revenue management and is there a potential for revenue management in the manufacturing industries? It turns out that a significant portion of manufacturing companies fulfill the requirements of successfully applying revenue management while only a small portion of the companies surveyed already apply revenue management in one way or the other. Thus, the need for theoretical decision models arises which could be used in the not-too-distant future to actually implement sophisticated revenue management systems for these manufacturing companies. Figure 1.1 sketches such a revenue management system.

© Springer Fachmedien Wiesbaden GmbH, part of Springer Nature 2009
F. Defregger, *Revenue Management for Manufacturing Companies*, Edition KWV,
https://doi.org/10.1007/978-3-658-24037-0_1

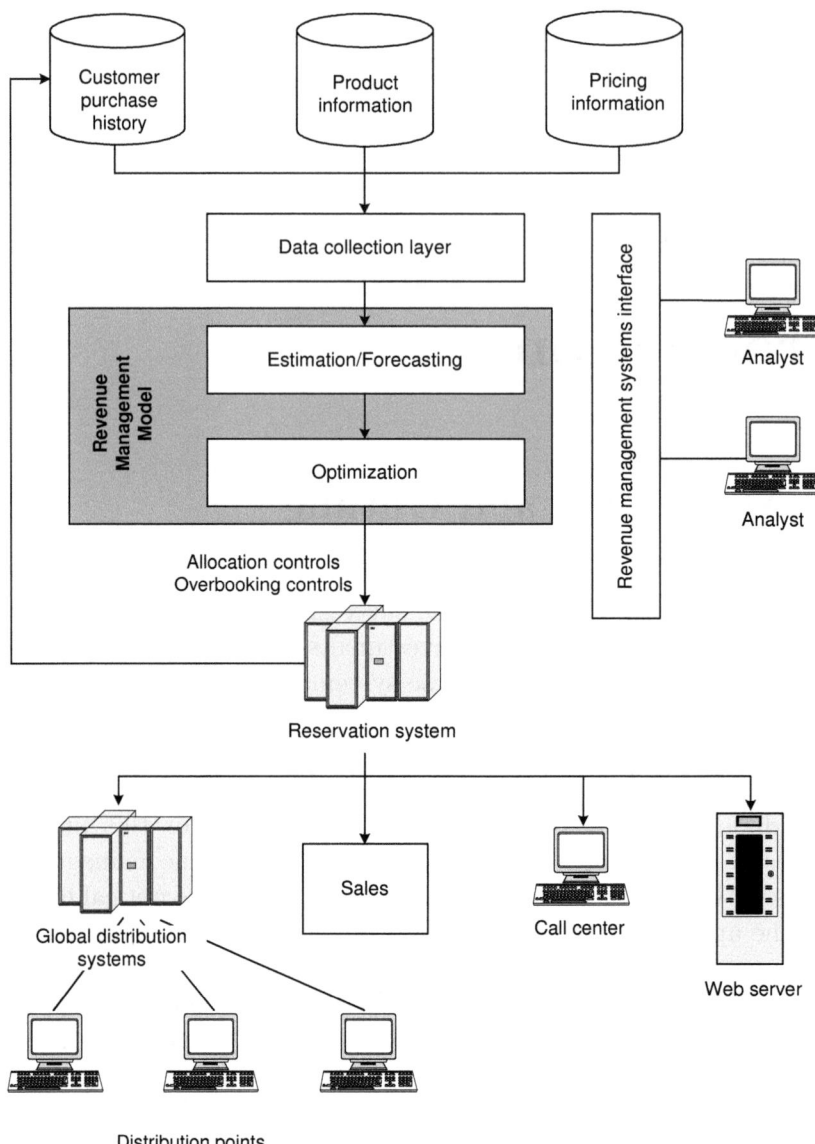

Figure 1.1: Revenue management system, following Talluri and van Ryzin (2004)

Data inputs into the revenue management system are the customer purchase history as well as product and pricing information. The input data is gathered in a data collection layer which feeds the quantitative revenue management model. The revenue management model mainly consists of two parts, namely an estimation and forecasting component and an optimization component. The output of the revenue management model is fed into the central reservation system. Thus, a company effectively controls its capacity by using a quantitative revenue management model. Calculations of the revenue management model are controlled by analysts who also have the possibility to set parameters of the model. The capacity of the company is then sold via different distribution channels, such as global distribution systems, a sales department, call centers or web servers.

The next chapters describe quantitative revenue management models for manufacturing companies and propose solution procedures to solve these models for large problem instances. All mathematical models in the next chapters are primarily concerned with the optimization routine of a revenue management system, see figure 1.1.

In Chapter 3, a basic quantitative model for revenue management at a manufacturing company is presented. After different solution procedures for evaluating policies and solving the model optimally have been compared with regards to their running times, a heuristic solution procedure is described which is able to produce significant improvements for large problem instances.

In chapter 4, the basic quantitative model is expanded by the use of a finished product inventory because usually manufacturing companies use the possibility to store finished products in order to be able to fulfill short term demands which are usually more profitable than longer term demands. A heuristic procedure is described which first tackles the problem of finding a good maximum inventory level in the trade-off between inventory holding costs and the additional profits that can be generated by higher inventory levels which enable the company to accept more profitable orders. After a good maximum inventory level has been determined, the heuristic procedure tries to find a good revenue management policy by trying to find the optimal rejection level of less profitable orders.

In chapter 5, the basic model of revenue management is expanded by the possibility of significant setup times and costs. In many industries, companies offer different products which are produced on the same resources. This often leads to significant setup times and costs and poses the interesting research question in how far revenue management can be used to increase the profitability in these circumstances. A heuristic procedure is presented in this chapter as well and the numerical tests show that it performs quite satisfactorily for a wide range of problem instances.

The dissertation concludes with a summary and an outlook into further research opportunities.

1.2   Revenue Management

Revenue management originates from the airline industry. In the late 1970s, airlines started to offer early-bird discounts in order to optimize the capacity utilization of their flights. One decision problem that emerged immediately was how many seats should be sold at the early-bird rate while reserving enough seats for the customers who would book shortly before their departure and pay the full price. This decision problem spawned a wide-ranging scientific literature, see McGill and van Ryzin (1999), and started the era of yield management, which later became known as revenue management.

Today, revenue management has gained ground in a number of industries, see Talluri and van Ryzin (2004). In order to see what revenue management presently encompasses, consider the steps a company has to take until the benefits of revenue management can be reaped, see Wong, Koppelman, and Daskin (1993). These steps might slightly differ depending on the actual industry that the company is operating in.

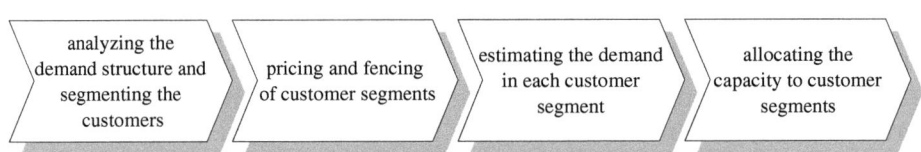

Figure 1.2: Phases of implementing revenue management

First, a company has to look at its demand structure and segment its customers by their willingness to pay. This is possible only if there exist differences in the customers' willingness to pay which is also a condition for using revenue management, see below. The result of the segmentation of customers will be two or more customer classes which differ in certain aspects of their demand, e.g. willingness to pay and service attributes of the product sold. An example for different customer classes would be the different cabin classes for a certain flight. Here, the customer classes usually differ by their willingness to pay and certain service attributes of a flight.

Once the customer classes have been segmented, they have to be priced according to the willingness to pay of the different customer classes. Furthermore, the company has to prevent that customers from higher-priced customer classes can buy the product from the lower-priced segment. In the airline industry, this is done by different measures, one of the more familiar ones being the restriction for tourists that there has to be a weekend between the dates of their outward and return flights. This way, business class passengers are discouraged to buy a ticket in the tourist class segment because business class passengers usually want to be home by the weekend.

After the customer segments have been developed, the stochastic demand in each customer segment has to be forecasted. These forecasts are then used to allocate the capacity of the company to the different customer segments.

A central decision problem of this capacity allocation process is to provide enough capacity for higher-priced segments while not crowding out too much lower-priced demand. If not enough capacity has been allocated for the higher-priced demand, the company loses revenue because it could have accepted more higher-priced demand if it had not accepted so much lower-priced demand. If, on the other hand, the company reserves too much capacity for higher-priced customer segments, it will lose revenue because it could have filled this capacity with demand from the lower-priced customer segments.

Compared to service industries, the operating conditions of manufacturing companies differ greatly for implementing capacity controls. Thus, in this dissertation new models and solution procedures for implementing capacity controls for manufacturing companies with the goal of profit maximization are considered.

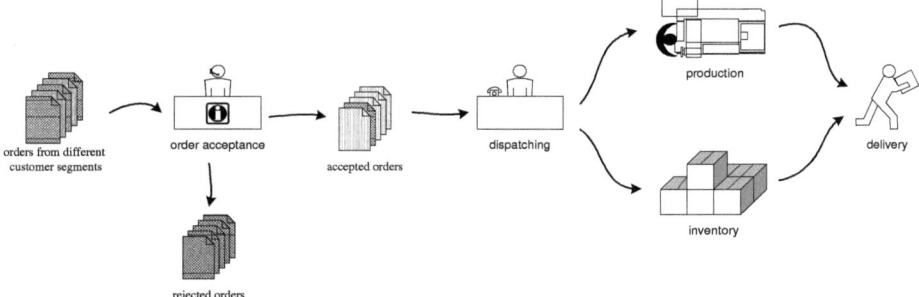

Figure 1.3: Capacity control at a manufacturing company

Figure 1.3 shows how the capacity control step of revenue management could be implemented at a manufacturing company. Orders from different customer classes arrive and are either accepted or rejected in order to reserve capacity for more profitable orders. All accepted orders are then scheduled into the production system and maybe partially or completely fulfilled from an inventory.

In order to utilize the benefits of revenue management, a number of conditions has to be met which are outlined below, see e.g. Kimes (1989).

First, the customers of a company have to have a different willingness to pay. In order to create this different willingness to pay, the company has to be able to find product differentiations which evoke a different willingness to pay on part of the customers. These product differentiations can be generated by physical or intangible product attributes. An example for a physical product differentiation would be different quality levels of a product. In the area of revenue management it is common to consider intangible product differentiations, e.g. the time between the customers decision to buy and the customer receiving the product or using the service. In the airline industry it is common to reserve capacity for high-paying business class passengers who only book a very short time before departure of the flight. For a manufacturing company, the lead time to deliver a product could constitute such a product differentiation. Customers who need the product urgently are more likely to have a higher willingness to pay than customers who can wait a bit longer to receive the product.

A second condition for utilizing the benefits of revenue management is a stochastic customer demand. If the customer demand would not be stochastic but rather deterministic, the company could decide in advance which customers it should accept and which customers to reject and no sophisticated capacity allocation techniques which constitute a major component of revenue management would be necessary.

A condition on the side of the company are inflexible capacities which can not always match the demand that the company encounters. If the capacity would be flexible enough to match any demand, the company could accept all customers and would not have to select which customers to sell their product or service for each point in time.

The last condition that has to be met is concerned with the perishability of the products or services that the company provides. If the company could store its supply in advance of the customer demand, the company could match its supply to the customer demand once it arrives. In the case of a service company it becomes clear that this condition is easily fulfilled as services can not be stored and are thus perishable. In the case of manufacturing companies this condition can be fulfilled by the fact that inventory capacities can be limited in the face of strong demand. Make-to-order companies fulfill this condition because they do not produce for an inventory, and thus their production capacity is perishable.

1.3 Literature Review

The scientific literature on revenue management is extensive. For a comprehensive overview of the literature especially in the non-manufacturing sectors see McGill and van Ryzin (1999) and Talluri and van Ryzin (2004). When looking at revenue management for the manufacturing industries, no comprehensive literature review exists as yet, so one will be given subsequently.

When optimizing the capacity allocation in a manufacturing context, it becomes clear that instead of accepting or rejecting passengers the acceptance or rejection of manufacturing orders placed by customers becomes relevant. Thus, a high portion of the relevant literature deals with the decision problem of how many and which orders should be accepted over a finite or infinite time horizon in a stochastic environment with the optimization criterion of maximizing profits.

Within the order acceptance literature, a number of authors model the decision problem with Markov decision processes. Miller (1969) considers the problem of profit-maximizing admission control to a queue which is basically equivalent to the order acceptance problem. Miller models the problem by a continuous-time Markov decision process and provides a specialized solution algorithm for the problem that he considers. Lippman and Ross (1971) extend Miller's model by allowing service times that are dependent on the customer classes, a general arrival process and an infinite number of customer classes and study this problem with a semi-Markov decision process. Lippman (1975) considers maximizing the average reward for a controlled $M/M/c$ queue, adapts a new definition for the transition times in Markov decision processes and is able to derive several important results. Matsui (1982, 1985) uses semi-Markov decision processes to consider several order selection policies for stochastic job shops with the goal of maximizing the long-term average reward. Carr and Duenyas (2000) use a continuous-time Markov decision process to model a combined make-to-stock/make-to-order manufacturing system in order to decide which orders should be accepted and how many make-to-stock products to make. The authors are able to find the structure of optimal control and sequencing policies. Kniker and Burman (2001) propose a discrete-time Markov decision process for order acceptance at a make-to-order company and Defregger and Kuhn (2004) outline a heuristic for this approach. In an extension of their earlier paper, Defregger and Kuhn (2007) provide a heuristic procedure for revenue management at a manufacturing company with the possibility to store its finished goods in an inventory.

Other modelling concepts for profit-maximizing order acceptance decisions in a stochastic manufacturing context have been used. Keilson (1970) and Balachandran and Schaefer (1981) provide nonlinear programming models and solution procedures for the order acceptance problem. In a series of papers, Balakrishnan, Patterson and Sridharan (1996,1999) and Patterson, Balakrishnan, and Sridharan (1997) use a decision-theoretic approach for reserving capacity of a make-to-order firm for orders with high profit margins. Caldentey (2001) approximates the order acceptance problem with a dynamic diffusion control model. In his model the price that the customers are willing to pay changes stochastically over time and the company has to decide about order acceptance and setting the inventory level. Missbauer (2003) uses a stochastic model to derive optimal lower bounds for the profit margin of stochastically arriving orders. Only orders whose contribution margins exceed the optimal lower bounds are accepted. Barut and Sridharan (2005) propose a heuristic procedure based on a decision tree analysis in order to determine amounts of consumable capacity for each order class that can be used to accept orders of this class.

While direct order acceptance and rejection is an important technique for controlling the capacity of a manufacturing company, there are other possibilities as well. By using these possibilities, a company tries to influence external demand for the products by changing prices or quoted due dates. One possibility is the concept of dynamic pricing. Instead of directly accepting or rejecting certain orders the company can dynamically change the price for a certain product over time, thus in effect rejecting more orders when raising the price and accepting more orders when lowering the price.

Low (1974) studies a semi-Markov decision process for determining optimal pricing policies for a $M/M/c$ queue. Harris and Pinder (1995) consider an assemble-to-order manufacturing company and determine optimal pricing and capacity reallocation policies for a static revenue management problem with an arbitrary number of customer classes. Gallego and van Ryzin (1997) consider pricing a given set of inventories of components that go into finished products over a finite time horizon. Swann (1999, 2001) examines the suitability of dynamic pricing in a manufacturing context and analyzes different dynamic pricing models. Chen and Frank (2001) analyze pricing policies for a company with homogeneous or heterogeneous customers where prices for admission to the queue depend on the size of the queue. Elimam and Dodin (2001) use nonlinear programming in order to determine optimal price discount levels during off-peak periods at a manufacturing company. Chan, Simchi-Levi, and Swann (2003) consider dynamic pricing strategies in a finite horizon problem under non-stationary, stochastic demand. Ziya, Hayriye, and Foley (2006) investigate optimal prices for $M/M/1/m$ and $M/GI/s/s$ blocking systems.

Besides dynamic pricing, companies can also control their capacity by quoting different due dates to customers. By quoting longer due dates the company can decrease external demand and is thus effectively rejecting more orders, while quoting shorter due dates increases the demand. Duenyas (1995) and Duenyas and Hopp (1995) use semi-Markov decision processes to solve the problem of quoting optimal lead times to customers when the probability of a customer placing an order depends on the lead time quoted to him. Easton and Moodie (1999) develop a probabilistic model in order to determine optimal pricing and due date setting decisions and Watanapa and Techanitisawad (2005) extend Easton and Moodie's model. Kapuscinski and Tayur (2000) are able to determine the structure of an optimal due date setting policy for a revenue management problem at a make-to-order company. Keskinocak, Ravi, and Tayur (2001) study several online and offline algorithms for quoting lead times to different customer classes where revenues obtained from the customers are sensitive to lead time.

For a literature review with mostly finite-horizon models on coordinating pricing with inventory and production decisions, see Chan, Shen, Simchi-Levi, and Swann (2004). If customers do not require an immediate reply whether their order will be accepted or not, the production capacity can also be auctioned off, see Gallien and Wein (2005) or Baker and Murthy (2005).

Chapter 2

Empirical Study

2.1 Overview

An empirical study was conducted to answer three research questions concerning the current state of revenue management in the German paper, steel and aluminium industries:

- What proportion of companies in these three sectors currently uses revenue management?

- What proportion of companies in the three sectors could potentially use revenue management in order to boost their profits?

- Does the size of a company have an influence on the answer of the first two research questions?

To answer these questions, questionnaires were sent to 311 companies in Germany. The paper, steel and aluminium industries were chosen because it is assumed that companies in these sectors are more likely than not to fulfill one of the conditions to use revenue management profitably, which is to have a relatively fixed capacity. 87 companies belong to the aluminium industry, 141 companies belong to the paper industry and 83 companies belong to the steel industry.

Before starting the real study, a pre-test was conducted with 27 randomly selected companies in order to obtain an estimate of the response rate and to assert that all questions were understood correctly by the companies. 6 companies answered, resulting in a satisfactory response rate of 22%. The

© Springer Fachmedien Wiesbaden GmbH, part of Springer Nature 2009
F. Defregger, *Revenue Management for Manufacturing Companies*, Edition KWV,
https://doi.org/10.1007/978-3-658-24037-0_2

questionnaire underwent minor modifications and was sent to the remaining 284 companies. 74 companies responded and after sending a reminder letter 33 more companies answered, resulting in a response rate of 38%.

The three research questions mentioned above were not asked directly in the questionnaire, but were rather modeled by a set of additional research questions. These additional research questions were then formed into written questions that were asked directly in the questionnaire. All answers to a research question were then recorded as the percentage proportion of the companies who answered the question positively. As the population of this empirical study is finite, these percentage proportions are governed by a hypergeometric distribution. The sample size for these hypergeometric distributions is given by the 107 companies which answered the questionnaire while the population is 284 companies. Some companies did not answer all questions of the questionnaire so that for these questions the sample size is less than 107. These questions will be marked accordingly.

In addition to the estimated proportions of the positive answers for each research question the confidence intervals for these proportion estimators were calculated by the method of Wendell and Schmee (2001) using the statistical system R, see R Development Core Team (2007). The overall confidence level that the true proportions lie in their respective confidence intervals was set to 90%. As there are 19 proportion estimators overall, the confidence level for a single confidence interval can be calculated by Boole's inequality which is mistakenly known as Bonferroni's inequality, see Seneta (1993). Boole's inequality states that the probability that all confidence intervals C_s simultaneously contain their respective true proportions μ_s satisfies

$$P(\mu_s \in C_s, \forall s \in \{1, \ldots, 19\}) \geq 1 - \sum_{s=1}^{19} \alpha_s$$

where C_s is a confidence interval for the proportion μ_s with a confidence level of $1 - \alpha_s$, see Law and Kelton (2000). As the probability P is set to 90% and each of the 19 confidence intervals is set to have the same level of confidence, the confidence level $1 - \alpha_s$ of each of the 19 confidence intervals can be calculated by

$$0.9 = 1 - 19\alpha_s \Leftrightarrow \alpha_s = \frac{0.1}{19} \Leftrightarrow 1 - \alpha_s \approx 99.5\%$$

Thus, when calculating the individual confidence intervals by the method of Wendell and Schmee (2001), an individual confidence level of $\alpha_s = 0.5\%$ was used.

2.2 Companies Using Revenue Management

To answer the question if a certain company is currently using revenue management, the following research questions were formulated:

(1) Does the company segment its customers?

(2) Does the company use price differentiation for its custom segments?

(3) Does the company regularly use forecasts?

(4) Does the company use revenue management capacity allocation techniques?

As question (4) can not be asked directly from a company, this question is represented by the following three questions:

(4.1) Does the company sometimes reject orders even if it could accept them, in the hope that a more lucrative order would arrive?

(4.2) Does the company demand higher prices for urgent orders?

(4.3) Does the company vary its prices depending on the current capacity utilization?

If one of these three questions is answered with a "yes", one can assume that the company allocates its capacity in a revenue management manner. Figure 2.1 shows the proportions of positive answers for question (4) and its derived questions (4.1) through (4.3) with the 99.5% confidence intervals. It can be seen that about 6% of the companies sometimes reject orders in the hope that more lucrative orders would arrive. About 10% of the companies demand higher prices for urgent orders and about 6% vary their prices depending on the current capacity utilization. Overall almost 20% of the companies fulfill one of the three criteria (4.1) through (4.3) and can thus be classified as using capacity allocation techniques in a revenue management manner.

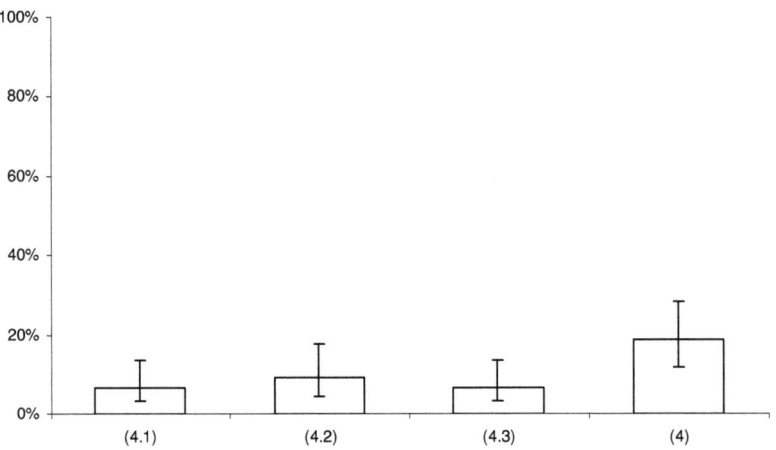

Figure 2.1: Proportion of companies that use capacity allocation

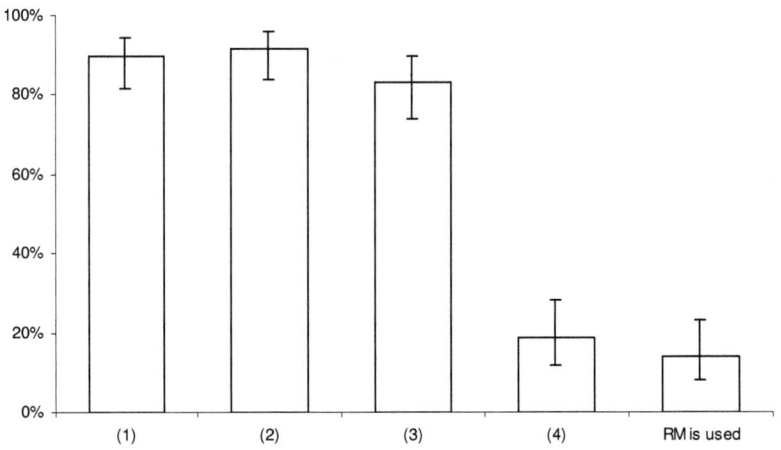

Figure 2.2: Proportion of companies that use revenue management

Figure 2.2 shows the proportions for answers (1) to (4) and the resulting proportion of companies who currently use revenue management which is assumed to be the case if all questions (1) to (4) was answered positively. It can be seen that most companies segment their customers, use price differentiation among those segments and regularly use forecasts. Thus, overall about 14% of the companies questioned currently use revenue management.

2.3 Potential of Revenue Management

To answer the question if a company has the potential for profitably using revenue management the following questions were asked:

(1) Can the company segment its customers?

(2) Is the customer demand stochastic?

(3) Does the company have inflexible production capacities?

(4) Does the company have perishable production capacities?

For the question if the company can segment its customers the companies were asked about how long the average time is between receiving an order and the latest possible production start to fulfill this order. The answer to this question is depicted in figure 2.3.

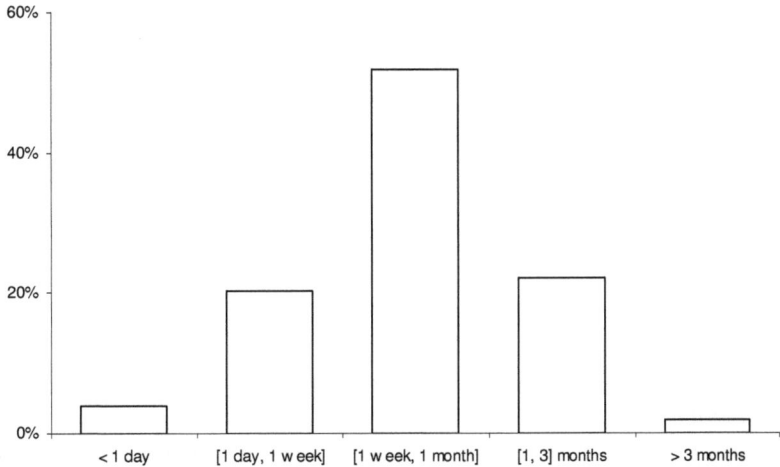

Figure 2.3: Distribution of the average time between receiving an order and the latest possible production start to fulfill that order

Figure 2.3 shows the hypergeometric distribution of the time range mentioned. Confidence intervals for a multidimensional hypergeometric distribution are not available. It can be seen that only at about 4% of the 104 companies who answered this question the time range was less than 1 day. Thus, 96% of the companies have the possibility to classify their customers according to the lead time wanted by a customer. In order to be able to segment the customers, a company has to have a minimum number of different customers. Thus, the companies were asked if they receive orders from more than 10 different customers regularly. This was the case for 105 out of 106 companies who answered this question. Overall, 98 of 103 and thus 95% of the companies who answered both questions had more than 10 customers and a time range between receiving an order and the latest possible start date for production of the order of more than 1 day. Thus, about 95% of the companies questioned can segment their customers.

To answer question (2) if customer demand is stochastic the companies were asked if unexpected orders arrive at the company from time to time. This was the case at 106 of the 107 companies who answered this question.

To answer question (3) if a company has inflexible production capacities, two indirect criteria were measured:

(3.1) Does the company have the possibility to order extra hours of work or can orders be outsourced to subcontractors if the company's production capacity is fully utilized?

(3.2) Does the company need more than 1 month to expand its own production capacities?

If the first criterion is answered negatively and the second criterion is answered positively one can assume that the production capacities of the company are fixed. Figure 2.4 shows the results of questions (3.1), (3.2) and (3). It can be seen that about 67% of the companies answered question (3.1) negatively and 105 out of 107 companies answered question (3.2) positively. Thus it can be concluded that about 2 thirds of the companies surveyed have inflexible production capacities.

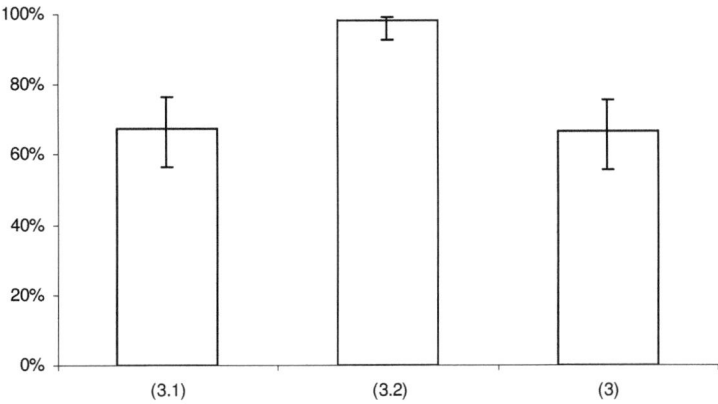

Figure 2.4: Proportion of companies with inflexible production capacities

To answer question (4) if a company has perishable production capacities, the following criteria were developed:

(4.1) Does the company produce without an inventory?

(4.2) Is the inventory capacity usually too scarce?

(4.3) Does the company start production only after receiving an order for a significant share of all orders?

If one of the three criteria is met one can assume that the production capacity of the company is perishable. Figure 2.5 shows the results for question (4.1), (4.2) and (4). About 9% of the 106 companies who answered this question have no inventory. About 43% of the 99 companies that answered this question have scarce inventory capacities and about 81% of the 105 companies that answered this question have a significant shares of orders that are produced in a make-to-order manner. Overall about 90% of the companies that answered one of these questions have perishable capacities.

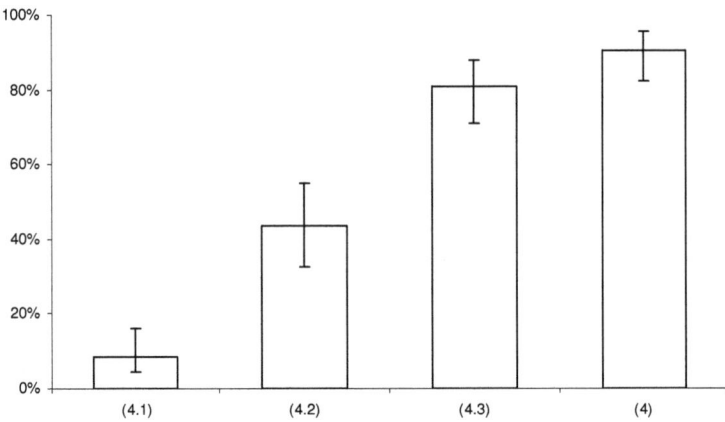

Figure 2.5: Proportion of companies with perishable production capacities

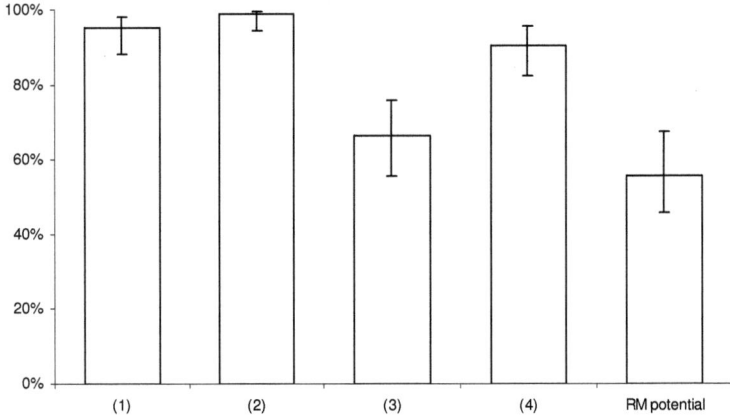

Figure 2.6: Proportion of the companies which fulfill the conditions to use revenue management

In conclusion, figure 2.6 shows the estimated proportions of the conditions for the companies to use revenue management in a profitable manner. Overall, about 56% of the companies have the potential to use revenue management. On the other hand, about 47% of the companies with a potential to do so do not use revenue management. This shows that these companies should at least seriously consider to introduce a revenue management system.

2.4 Influence of the Size of a Company

The third research question is concerned with the influence of the size of a company on the actual and potential use of revenue management. This research question was examined by contingency tables, see Agresti (2002). The size of a company was measured by the number of people employed at that company. A company was classified as small if its number of employees fell into the $[0, 49]$ interval, as medium-sized if its number of employees fell into the $[50, 499]$ interval and as large if its number of employees fell into the $[500, \infty]$ interval. Out of the 107 companies that answered the questionnaire, there were 7 small companies, 64 medium-sized companies and 36 large companies. Denote by U the size of a company, where U can take one of the values "small", "medium" or "large". Denote by W the variable that a company currently uses revenue management and by O the variable that a company has the potential for using revenue management. Table 2.1 shows the contingency table for the variables U and W.

	small	medium	large	$\sum$
revenue management is used	0	8	7	15
revenue management is not used	7	56	29	92
	7	64	36	107

Table 2.1: Contingency table for the influence of the size of a company on whether it uses revenue management or not

It can be seen that no small company currently uses revenue management, while 8 out of 64 medium-sized companies and 7 out of 36 large companies currently use revenue management. These proportions are depicted in figure 2.7.

While figure 2.7 seems to suggest that the size of a company has an influence on whether it is currently using revenue management or not this

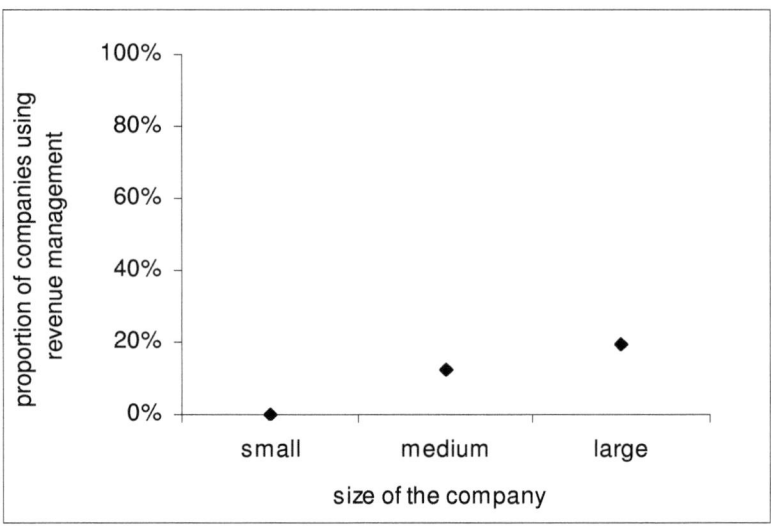

Figure 2.7: Proportions of the companies which use revenue management

assumption can not be validated statistically. The significance level of a statistical test is the maximum probability of falsely rejecting a true null hypothesis. The p-value is the smallest significance level at which the null hypothesis would be rejected for a given observation, see Conover (1999). As the null hypothesis is rejected if the calculated p-value is smaller than the significance level chosen by the researcher, a low p-value gives strong evidence that the null hypothesis of a statistical test can be rejected. A significance level of 0.05 was chosen for all statistical tests.

In order to test for the independence of the variables U and W, the chi-square test is employed which results in a p-value of 0.3425. This shows that the null hypothesis that the variables U and W are independent can not be rejected at a significance level of 0.05 and it can not be demonstrated that the size of a company has an influence on whether that company uses revenue management. This is confirmed by the relatively low value of 0.142 for the association measure of Cramér which can be viewed as a coefficient of correlation for nominal data, see Agresti (2002).

When looking at the influence of the size of a company on its potential to use revenue management a different picture emerges. Table 2.2 shows the contingency table for the variable U and O.

Figure 2.8 shows that almost half of the small and medium-sized com-

	small	medium	large	$\sum$
potential for revenue management	3	28	27	58
no potential for revenue management	4	35	7	46
	7	63	34	104

Table 2.2: Contingency table for the influence of the size of a company on its potential to use revenue management

panies have the potential to use revenue management while almost 80% of the large companies have this potential. Using the chi-square test a p-value of 0.0033 emerges so the null hypothesis of independence of the variables U and O can be rejected. Thus, one can say that the size of a company has an influence whether a company can successfully use revenue management. According to the data, larger companies have a greater potential for revenue management than smaller companies. This is confirmed by Cramér's association measure which takes a value of 0.332.

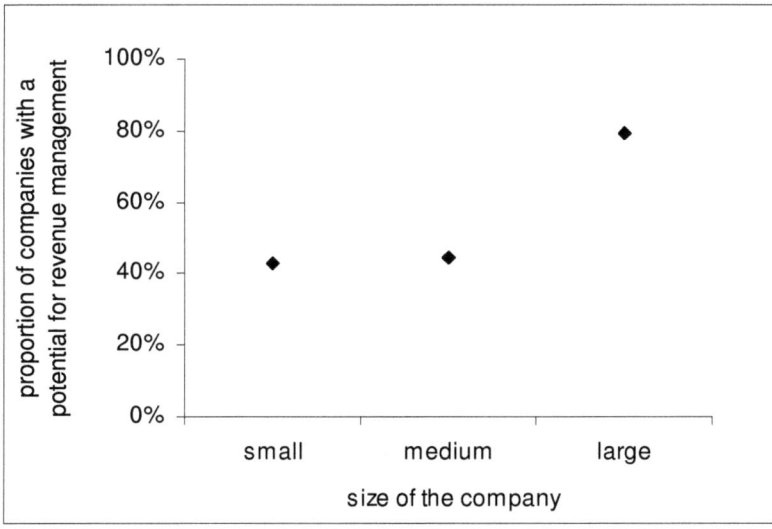

Figure 2.8: Proportions of the companies which have the potential for revenue management

Overall, one can say that the size of a company does not have any influence on whether the company is currently using revenue management but larger companies seem to have a greater potential for making use of revenue management than smaller companies. Kuhn and Defregger (2005) give a more elaborate discussion of the empirical study.

Chapter 3

Basic Model

In this chapter a basic quantitative model for applying revenue management to a manufacturing company is presented, following the paper of Kniker and Burman (2001). Furthermore, we compare different solution procedures for evaluating a policy and solving the decision model and we present a heuristic procedure for solving the decision model. Numerical results show that applying revenue management can have a distinct advantage over a simple first-come-first-served (FCFS) policy and that the heuristic procedure is useful for finding good policies for large problem instances.

3.1 Model

In this section the decision model is described. After presenting the model assumptions and formulating the model, the model is classified. The classification is necessary in order to find the correct solution procedures that can solve the model. At the end of this section, the procedure to create individual problem instances is described.

3.1.1 Model Assumptions

Consider a make-to-order company with one machine and one or more product types. Orders of different order classes arrive at the company. Each product type can encompass one or more order classes. The order classes differentiate the orders by their profit margins, lead times, processing times and arrival probabilities. The company has to decide which orders to accept

© Springer Fachmedien Wiesbaden GmbH, part of Springer Nature 2009
F. Defregger, *Revenue Management for Manufacturing Companies*, Edition KWV,
https://doi.org/10.1007/978-3-658-24037-0_3

and which orders to reject. It might be more profitable for the company not to accept all orders because if the company accepts all orders, the situation might arise that the company has to reject orders of order classes with higher profit margins because it accepted too many orders of order classes with lower profit margins. In this situation, the orders with lower profit margins crowd out the orders with higher profit margins and the company loses some profits. Thus, the company has to decide in which situations it should accept which order classes. If many orders have been accepted and not been processed yet, it might be wise only to accept orders with relatively high profit margins. If the current queue of accepted orders is empty, the situation is different. Here it might be profitable to accept any order which arrives at the company. The decision problem is depicted in figure 3.1.

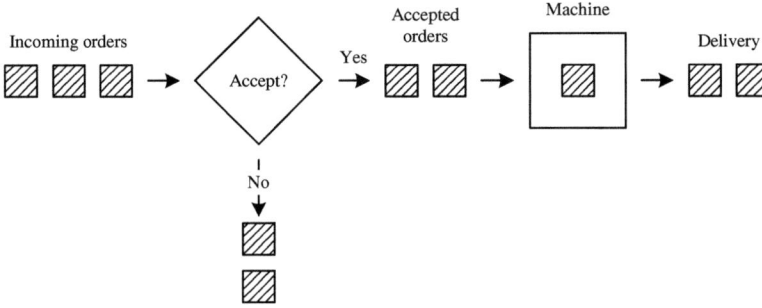

Figure 3.1: Basic decision problem

3.1.2   Model Formulation

The model is an infinite-horizon discrete-time Markov decision process which is characterized as follows. All orders arriving at the company belong to a certain order class $n \in \{1, \dots, N\}$. In each discrete time period at most one order of any class n can arrive with probability p_n, $\sum_{n=1}^{N} p_n < 1$. All orders of class n have a profit margin of m_n monetary units, a capacity usage of u_n discrete time periods and a lead time of l_n time periods. The lead time specifies that the customer is willing to wait for a maximum of l_n time periods when placing the order at the company. To model the case that no order arrives in a given period, the dummy order class $n = 0$ is used, $p_0 = 1 - \sum_{n=1}^{N} p_n$, $p_0 > 0$, $m_0 = u_0 = l_0 = 0$.

Each system state (n, c) is characterized by the two state variables n and c, where n is the order class of the order that has arrived at the beginning of the current period and c is the number of periods that the capacity is booked out by orders which have already been accepted and not been completed yet. The set of all system states (n, c) is denoted by S. The number of states $|S|$ for a certain problem instance is given by

$$|S| = (N + 1)\, l^{\max} \tag{3.1}$$

where $l^{\max}$, the maximum lead time, is given by $l^{\max} = \max_n l_n$. Each state has a set of decisions $D[(n, c)]$ which can be taken in that state. The state-dependent decisions D of the Markov decision process are given by

$$D[(n, c)] = \begin{cases} D1 := \text{"reject"} \\ D2 := \text{"accept"} : n > 0 \wedge c + u_n \leq l_n \end{cases}$$

Orders can always be rejected and in the case no order arrives $D1$ has the meaning of "wait for the next order to arrive". An order can only be accepted if an order has arrived $(n > 0)$ and the order can be finished within its lead time l_n. Action- and state-dependent rewards R are given by

$$R^{D1}[(n, c)] = 0, \ \forall (n, c) \in S$$
$$R^{D2}[(n, c)] = m_n, \ \forall (n, c) \in S$$

The company receives a reward of m_n if it accepts an order of class n, otherwise there is no reward. The transition probabilities in the case of rejecting an order are:

$$P^{D1}[(n, c), (m, \max\{c - 1, 0\})] = p_m, \forall (n, c) \in S, \forall m \in \{0, \dots, N\}$$

By rejecting an order or waiting for the next order to arrive the capacity usage c is decreased by 1. If c has reached zero, it stays zero if the company continues to reject orders or no orders arrive. The transition probabilities for accepting an order are:

$$P^{D2}[(n, c), (m, c + u_n - 1)] = \begin{cases} p_m, & \forall (n, c) \in S, m \in \{0, \dots, N\} \\ 0, & \text{else} \end{cases}$$

When accepting an order, c is increased by u_n, but c will be decreased by one unit by the beginning of the next period because of the ongoing production. Thus, c can range between 0 and $c^{\text{max}} = l^{\text{max}} - 1$. By solving the Markov decision process an optimality criterion is optimized by finding the optimal policy π^{opt} which maps an optimal decision to each state (n, c).

With regards to the optimality criterion of the Markov decision process we follow the recommendation of Puterman (1994). He recommends using the average reward per period for the optimality criterion when decisions are made frequently which is the case here.

3.1.3   Model Classification

Before a solution procedure to solve the Markov decision process can be applied, the Markov decision process has to be classified. As we will show, this Markov decision process can be classified as unichain. According to Puterman (1994), a Markov decision process can be classified as unichain if the transition matrix to every deterministic policy consists of a single recurrent class plus a possibly empty set of transient states. A state is classified as recurrent if there is a positive probability that the stochastic process will return to this state time if the stochastic process currently is in this state.

In order to show that the Markov decision process is unichain, the two state variables n and c have to be considered. First, consider the state variable n. In every period, any order of class $n \in \{1, \dots, N\}$ can arrive so the Markov decision process will always be unichain with regards to the state variable n.

With regards to the state variable c, it has to be shown that all capacity booking levels $c \in \{0, \dots, c^{\text{max}}\}$ can be reached under all policies whereby c^{max} can vary depending on the policy.

For a FCFS policy which accepts all orders whenever possible, $c^{\text{max}} = l^{\text{max}} - 1$. For this policy one can see that all states (n, c) are recurrent under this policy because any capacity booking level $c \in \{0, \dots, c^{\text{max}}\}$ can be reached repeatedly over time. The capacity booking level can always reach its maximum c^{max} if every period an order arrives for an extended period of time. Furthermore, c can also reach its minimum of zero and stay there if no order arrives for a long period of time. As every state is accessible from every other state the transition matrix consists of a single recurrent class under this policy.

There are other policies where the maximum c^{max} that c can reach will be lower than $l^{\mathrm{max}} - 1$. This might be either due to policies that do not accept all order classes, specifically order class $n = \arg\max_n l_n$ or due to policies that accept all order classes but not in all capacity booking levels c where they could be accepted. In the case of such a policy one can see that all states (n, c) with $c > c^{\mathrm{max}}$ will be transient states and all states (n, c) with $c \leq c^{\mathrm{max}}$ will be recurrent states.

In conclusion, under any policy the resulting transition matrix consists of a single recurrent class plus a possibly empty set of transient states and the Markov decision process can accordingly be classified as unichain. It follows that in order to solve this Markov decision process, the unichain versions of the standard solution procedures can be applied.

3.1.4 Creating Problem Instances

As we compare different solution procedures to evaluate a given policy in the next section with a set of randomly created problem instances, the procedure to create an individual problem instance is presented here.

The input data to the routine that creates a single problem instance is the number of states $|S|$, the number of order classes N and the traffic intensity ρ which is given by $\rho = \sum_{n=1}^{N} p_n u_n$. The number of order classes N is drawn from a uniform distribution whose range depends on the number of states $|S|$. For example, when comparing different evaluation and solution procedures of Markov decision processes, the number of states is set to 10,000 and the range of the uniform distribution for the number of order classes is set to $[5, 30]$.

Once the number of order classes N and the traffic intensity ρ have been determined for a certain problem instance, the maximum lead time l^{max} can be calculated by

$$l^{\mathrm{max}} = \lfloor |S|/(N+1) \rfloor \tag{3.2}$$

see equation (3.1). The real number of states that the problem instance will have is calculated by

$$|S|^{\mathrm{real}} = l^{\mathrm{max}}(N+1).$$

$|S|^{\mathrm{real}}$ will often differ marginally from the number of states $|S|$ that was originally planned for the problem instance because $|S|$, l^{max} and N all have to be integer numbers.

After l^{max} and $|S|^{\mathrm{real}}$ have been calculated, for each order class $n \in \{1, \ldots, N\}$ the routine randomly draws the share σ_n in the traffic intensity ρ, where $\sum_{n=1}^{N} \sigma_n = 1$. One possibility would be to give each order class an equal share of $\sigma_n = 1/N$, but in order to account for more diverse distributions of the σ_n, they are drawn by the following procedure.

Algorithm 3.1 Draw shares σ_n in the traffic intensity

---

draw $\underline{\sigma} \sim U[\frac{0.01}{N}, \frac{1}{N}]$

$\overline{\sigma} \leftarrow 1 - (N-1)\underline{\sigma}$

$\overline{\sigma}_v \leftarrow \overline{\sigma}$

for $n = 1$ to $N - 1$ **do**

    draw $\sigma_n \sim U[\underline{\sigma}, \overline{\sigma}_v]$

    $\overline{\sigma}_v \leftarrow \min\{1 - \sum_{m=1}^{n} s_m - (N - 1 - n)\underline{\sigma}, \overline{\sigma}\}$

end for

$s_N \leftarrow 1 - \sum_{n=1}^{N-1} \sigma_n$

First, a global lower bound $\underline{\sigma}$ for all σ_n is drawn from a uniform $[0.01/N, 1/N]$ distribution. If $\underline{\sigma}$ is drawn to be near $1/N$, then most σ_n will be near $1/N$ and each order class will have a similar share of the overall traffic intensity. On the other hand, if $\underline{\sigma}$ is drawn to be near $0.01/N$, the shares of the traffic intensities can have a much higher variance. The possible variation of $\underline{\sigma}$ ensures the possibility of a large number of different distributions of the shares σ_n.

After $\underline{\sigma}$ has been drawn, a global upper bound $\overline{\sigma}$ for all $\sigma_n, n \in \{1, \ldots, N-1\}$ is calculated by $\overline{\sigma} = 1 - (N-1)\underline{\sigma}$. A variable upper bound $\overline{\sigma}_v$ is initialized with the global upper bound $\overline{\sigma}$. Then, for each order class $n \in \{1, \ldots, N-1\}$ a share in the traffic intensity is drawn from a uniform $[\underline{\sigma}, \overline{\sigma}_v]$ distribution and the upper bound $\overline{\sigma}_v$ is updated accordingly after each iteration. In the end, s_N is calculated by $1 - \sum_{n=1}^{N-1} \sigma_n$.

After the shares σ_n have been specified, the traffic intensity ρ_n of each order class n can be calculated by

$$\rho_n = \sigma_n \rho \tag{3.3}$$

and the order classes are sorted in ascending order by their traffic intensities ρ_n. After that, N capacity usages u_n are drawn from a uniform $[1, l^{\max}]$ distribution for each order class and sorted in ascending order as well. The ordered usages are matched to the ordered traffic intensities ρ_n. This matching of low usages with low order class traffic intensities and high usages with high order class traffic intensities is done to minimize extremely low probabilities p_n which can cause numerical instabilities.

Now the arrival probability p_n for every order class can be calculated by $p_n = \rho_n / u_n$. The probability p_0 that no order arrives in a period is calculated by $p_0 = 1 - \sum_{n=1}^{N} p_n$. Subsequently, the lead time l_n of each order class n is drawn from a $[u_n, l^{\max}]$ uniform distribution. Then the relative profit margin m_n^{rel} for each order class $n \in 1, \ldots, N$ is drawn. The relative profit margins are drawn instead of the profit margins m_n because order classes can be better compared by their relative profit margins instead of their profit margins. The relative profit margins are drawn from a $[1,5]$ left triangular distribution, see figure 3.2. The left triangular distribution was chosen because it is more likely that only a few order classes have a high relative profit margin while most order classes should have lower relative profit margins.

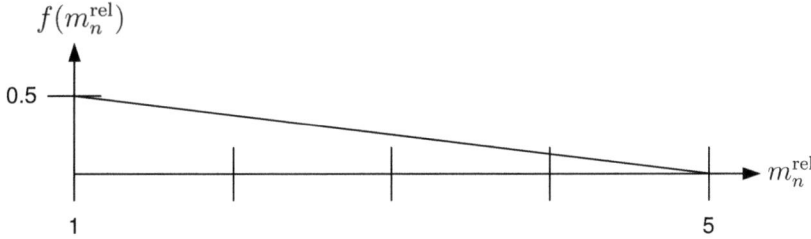

Figure 3.2: Density function of a left triangular $[1, 5]$ distribution

After the relative profit margins m_n^{rel} have been drawn, they are sorted in ascending order and matched to the N order classes which have been sorted by their lead times in descending order. This ensures that orders of classes with shorter lead times receive higher relative profit margins than orders of classes with longer lead times. In the end, the profit margin m_n can be calculated for each order class n from the relative profit margin by $m_n = u_n m_n^{\text{rel}}$.

In the next section, different solution procedures for evaluating the average reward of a given policy are presented. To compare them with respect to their running times, a number of problem instances are created by following the procedure that was described in this section.

3.2 Evaluating a Policy

A policy π is a rule which specifies for each state $i \in S$ which decision $d \in D(i)$ should be taken once the system enters state i. A policy is called a stationary policy if the decision to be taken in each state does not vary over time. We only consider stationary policies. Once a policy π has been selected, the discrete-time Markov decision process reduces to a discrete-time Markov reward process with transition probabilities $P^\pi(i, j)$ from state i to state j and rewards $R^\pi(i)$ that the decision maker receives when leaving state i under the given policy π. In order to compare different policies one has to evaluate the average reward per period $g(\pi)$ that results from a certain policy π. In the following, we describe four solution procedures to evaluate the average reward $g(\pi)$ of a given policy π for a unichain Markov decision process, for a reference see Puterman (1994) or Tijms (1994). At the end of this section, the procedures to evaluate a given policy are compared with respect to their running times.

3.2.1 Evaluation Equations

One possibility to evaluate the average reward $g(\pi)$ is to solve the evaluation equations which are given by the linear system of equations

$$g(\pi) + v(i) - \sum_{j \in S} P^\pi(i, j)\, v(j) = R^\pi(i), \forall i \in S \qquad (3.4)$$

where $P^\pi(i, j)$ denotes the transition probability from state i to state j and $R^\pi(i)$ denotes the reward the decision-maker receives when leaving state i under policy π. The components $v(i)$ represent relative values between states. The difference between the relative values of two states i and j, $v(i) - v(j)$, indicates the difference in the total expected reward if the stochastic process starts in state i and not in state j. For example, if $v(i) = 0$ and $v(j) = -10$ and the Markov reward process starts in state i, the decision maker will have 10 monetary units more overall than if the process would have started in state j. In contrast, the average reward $g(\pi)$ is independent of the state that the system starts in, at least for the unichain Markov decision processes that are considered here.

As the system of equations (3.4) is under-determined, one of the components $v(i)$ has to be set to zero in order to solve the evaluation equations. In the case of the mathematical model described in section 3.1.2 we set the relative value of the state $(n = 0, c = 0)$, $v[(0,0)]$, to zero to obtain the following linear system of equations:

$$v[(0,0)] = 0 \qquad (3.5)$$

$$g(\pi) + v(i) - \sum_{j \in S} P^{\pi}(i,j)\, v(j) = R^{\pi}(i), \forall i \in S \qquad (3.6)$$

For solving linear systems of equations one can use direct or iterative methods. As the transition matrices of the Markov reward processes are large systems with a high percentage of zero entries, iterative methods are preferred in terms of both computer memory requirements and running times, see Burden and Faires (1997). The Gauss-Seidel iterative technique was used for solving the linear system of evaluation equations, for implementation considerations see Stewart (1994).

Usually one can use over-relaxation in order to speed up the Gauss-Seidel iterative technique, but over-relaxation did not work for the basic model described in section 3.1.2 because the iterative process diverged for unknown reasons.

Even when not using over-relaxation, the Gauss-Seidel iterative technique did not converge for the relative values of states which have the same relative value as state $(0,0)$, i.e. for states i where $v(i) = v[(0,0)] = 0$. Denote the set of these states by $S_{v=0}$. By using under-relaxation, the iterates of $v(i), i \in S_{v=0}$, converged, but we developed a different approach which makes it possible to forgo under-relaxation and thus results in faster computations.

This approach starts by identifying all states in the set $S_{v=0}$ and then using a special convergence test for the iterates of $v(i), i \in S_{v=0}$. The states $i \in S_{v=0}$ can be identified by the following property:

$$i \in S_{v=0} \Leftrightarrow v(i) = v[(0,0)] = 0 \Leftrightarrow (c = 0 \vee c = 1) \wedge R^{\pi}(i) = 0 \qquad (3.7)$$

This means a state has the same relative and thus economic value as state $(0,0)$ if it models a current capacity usage of either 0 or 1 and if no reward is obtained when entering this state under policy π. Property (3.7) can be explained by the fact that no reward can be collected in state $(0,0)$ because no order has arrived in this state and that the state $(0,0)$ will inevitably transition to a state where the capacity usage c stays 0. This transition to a state with $c = 0$ can only happen from a state with $c = 0$ or $c = 1$ and in which no order is accepted and consequently no reward is received.

As the relative values $v(i), i \in S_{v=0}$ are known to equal $v[(0,0)] = 0$, the convergence test for these relative values is set to

$$|v(i)^{(k)}| < \beta, i \in S_{v=0}$$

where $v(i)^{(k)}$ is the iterate of $v(i)$ in iteration k and β is chosen to be 10^{-10}.

The convergence test for the relative values $v(j), j \notin S_{v=0}$ is given by

$$\frac{|v(j)^{(k)} - v(j)^{(k-1)}|}{|v(j)^{(k)}|} < \delta, j \notin S_{v=0}$$

where $v(j)^{(k)}$ is the iterate of $v(j)$ in iteration k and δ is chosen to be 10^{-5}. In order to validate the results of our implementation of the Gauss-Seidel iterative technique and to see if the equations could be solved faster, we also solved the linear system of evaluation equations by formulating it as a linear program and solving it with CPLEX 6.0. The linear program was implemented by setting equations (3.5) and (3.6) as constraints and maximizing $g(\pi)$. The results are presented in section 3.2.5.

3.2.2 Stationary Probabilities

The average reward $g(\pi)$ of a certain policy π can also be obtained by

$$g(\pi) = \sum_{i \in S} \tilde{P}^{\pi}(i) R^{\pi}(i)$$

where $\tilde{P}^{\pi}(i), i \in S$, is the stationary probability of state i resulting from the Markov reward process under policy π and $R^{\pi}(i)$ is the reward obtained in state i under policy π. The stationary probabilities $\tilde{P}^{\pi}(i)$ are obtained by the following system of equations:

$$\tilde{P}^\pi(j) \;=\; \sum_{i \in S} \tilde{P}^\pi(i)\, P^\pi(i,j), \forall j \in S \tag{3.8}$$

$$\sum_{i \in S} \tilde{P}^\pi(i) \;=\; 1 \tag{3.9}$$

In order to solve this system of linear equations the Gauss-Seidel iterative technique is used for equations (3.8) and the $\tilde{P}^\pi(i)$ are normalized after obtaining a solution.

The convergence test of all iterates $\tilde{P}^\pi(i)$ is given by

$$\frac{|\tilde{P}^\pi(i)^{(k)} - \tilde{P}^\pi(i)^{(k-1)}|}{|\tilde{P}^\pi(i)^{(k)}|} < \delta, \forall i \in S$$

where $\tilde{P}^\pi(i)^{(k)}$ is the iterate of $\tilde{P}^\pi(i)$ in iteration k and δ is chosen to be 10^{-5}. The system of linear equations (3.8) and (3.9) was also solved using CPLEX by formulating this system as constraints of a linear program with the objective function of maximizing the left-hand side of equation (3.9).

As the stationary probability distribution that CPLEX provides by directly implementing equations (3.8) and (3.9) is not exact enough for a large number of states $|S|$, equation (3.9) was replaced by

$$\sum_{i \in S} \tilde{P}^\pi(i) = |S|$$

and the $\tilde{P}(i)$ were normalized after obtaining the solution from CPLEX. This way, we were able to obtain an exact stationary probability distribution.

3.2.3 Simulation

A Markov reward process resulting from a certain policy can also be evaluated by simulation. Simulation can be implemented by starting out in a certain state, e.g. state $(0,0)$, and simulating the stochastic process that is governed by the Markov chain of the Markov reward process resulting from policy π. During each transition, the rewards that are received in the visited states are accumulated and at the end of a simulation replication the average reward per period can be estimated by dividing the accumulated average reward by the replication length. In order to estimate the average reward per period of a given policy, a number of such simulation replications has to be performed. The final result of simulating a certain policy π is an estimate $\widehat{g}(\pi)$ for the true average reward $g(\pi)$ of this policy as given by the following equation:

$$\widehat{g}(\pi) = \overline{X}_\pi(n) = \sum_{i=1}^{n} \frac{X_{\pi i}}{n}$$

where $\overline{X}_\pi(n)$ is the average of the average rewards $X_{\pi i}$ that are obtained in the replications $i \in \{1, \ldots, n\}$ when simulating policy π.

An approximate $100(1 - \alpha)$ percent confidence interval for $\overline{X}_\pi(n)$ is given by

$$\overline{X}_\pi(n) \pm t_{n-1,1-\alpha/2} \sqrt{\frac{S^2(n)}{n}}$$

where $t_{n-1,1-\alpha/2}$ is the upper $(1 - \alpha)/2$ critical point for the t distribution with $n - 1$ degrees of freedom and $S^2(n)$ is the sample variance of the $X_{\pi i}$ that were obtained by the n replications so far, see Law and Kelton (2000).

The number of replications to be made depends on the precision of the estimated average reward that one wants to obtain. A measure for this precision can be given by the relative error γ which is given by

$$\gamma = \frac{|\overline{X}_\pi(n) - g(\pi)|}{|g(\pi)|}$$

where $g(\pi)$ is the true average reward associated with policy π. In order to obtain an estimate of $g(\pi)$ with a maximum relative error of γ and a confidence level of $(1 - \alpha)$ one first makes a certain minimum number of replications and continues to make replications until

$$\frac{t_{n-1,1-\alpha/2} \sqrt{\frac{S^2(n)}{n}}}{\overline{X}_\pi(n)} \leq \frac{\gamma}{1 + \gamma} \quad ,$$

see Law and Kelton (2000). We set γ to 0.5% and α to 5% so one can be sure with an approximate confidence level of 95% that the estimated average reward $\widehat{g}(\pi)$ which is obtained in a given simulation run does not differ by more than 0.5% from the true average reward $g(\pi)$.

The replication length and the length of the warm-up period have to be set as well. To determine the length of the warm-up period the procedure of Welch is used, see Law and Kelton (2000).

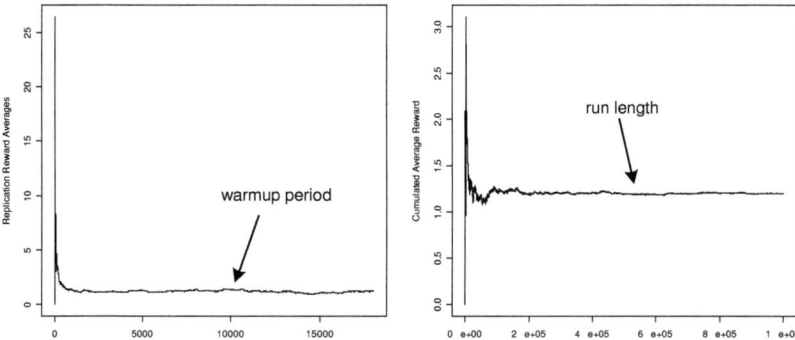

Figure 3.3: Procedure of Welch to determine the warmup period and procedure to determine the run length of a single replication

In order to determine the run length for a simulation run, a single pilot run is conducted with a warmup period that has been determined by the procedure of Welch. In this pilot run, the cumulated average reward per period is calculated for every period and graphically displayed, see figure 3.3. Similarly to the procedure of Welch, the run length for all replications is determined where the plot seems reasonably smooth.

One further parameter that has to be set before any simulation runs can take place is the minimum number of replications to be performed. Following Law and Kelton (2000), the minimum number of replications is set to ten.

The built-in random number generator of the programming environment that we used had only a period of $2^{24} - 1$. This was sometimes not enough to achieve a sufficiently high number of long replications to meet the maximum relative error of $\gamma = 0.5\%$. Consequently, we implemented the combined multiple recursive random number generator MRG32k3a. This random number generator has a period of about 2^{191} and better statistical properties, see L'Ecuyer (1999) and L'Ecuyer (2001).

3.2.4 Value Iteration

One of the standard methods for finding an optimal policy is the value iteration algorithm. This algorithm cannot only be used for solving a Markov decision process, however, but for evaluating a given policy π as well. This is detailed in algorithm 3.2.

Algorithm 3.2 Value iteration for evaluating a policy

$n \leftarrow 1$

$V_0(i) \leftarrow 0, \forall i \in S$

repeat

    1. compute for every state $i \in S$ the values $V_n(i)$ by

$$V_n(i) \leftarrow R^\pi(i) + \sum_{j \in S} P^\pi(i,j)V_{n-1}(j), \forall i \in S$$

    2. compute the bounds

$$\underline{\Delta V} \leftarrow \min_{i \in S}\{V_n(i) - V_{n-1}(i)\}$$

$$\overline{\Delta V} \leftarrow \max_{i \in S}\{V_n(i) - V_{n-1}(i)\}$$

    3. $n \leftarrow n + 1$

until $\overline{\Delta V} - \underline{\Delta V} \leq \epsilon \underline{\Delta V}$

obtain an estimate $\widehat{g}(\pi)$ for the average reward $g(\pi)$ by

$$\widehat{g}(\pi) \leftarrow \underline{\Delta V} + 0.5\left(\overline{\Delta V} - \underline{\Delta V}\right)$$

It can be seen that for each state $i \in S$ the values $V_n(i)$ are calculated during each iteration n. Each value $V_n(i)$ represents the value of state i if the stochastic process would end in n periods. The successive differences $V_n(i) - V_{n-1}(i)$ will eventually converge to the average reward $g(\pi)$ of the policy as the lower bound of the differences, $\underline{\Delta V}$, will continually increase and the upper bound $\overline{\Delta V}$ will continually decrease. Value iteration can only approximate the true average reward $g(\pi)$ by its estimate $\widehat{g}(\pi)$ with an accuracy of ϵ, though. Similar to the relative error γ that is used in simulation, ϵ is set to 0.5%.

3.2.5 Comparing Procedures to Evaluate a Policy

In order to determine which solution procedure to evaluate a given policy is most suitable they are compared with respect to their running times.

3.2.5.1 Small Problem Instances

The solution procedures were compared with 100 problem instances, each instance with a problem size $|S|$ of 10,000 states. The number of order classes was drawn from a $[5, 30]$ uniform distribution for each problem instance and the traffic intensity from a $[1, 2.5]$ uniform distribution. For each problem instance, the FCFS policy which accepts all orders as long as they can be accepted was evaluated by each solution procedure on a 733 MHz Intel Pentium machine with 392 MB of memory and the running time to evaluate the FCFS policy was measured for each solution procedure.

In order to validate the correct implementation of the solution procedures, the average reward of each solution procedure was compared to the average reward of the solution procedure "Evaluation Equations (CPLEX)" for each problem instance. Table 3.1 shows the maximum over all 100 problem instances of the absolute percentage deviation from the solution procedure "Evaluation Equations (CPLEX)" for each of the other five solution procedures.

solution procedure	mean	maximum
evaluation equations (Gauss-Seidel)	0.00%	0.00%
stationary probabilities (Gauss-Seidel)	0.01%	0.12%
stationary probabilities (CPLEX)	0.00%	0.00%
simulation	0.21%	1.08%
value iteration	0.08%	0.20%

Table 3.1: Mean and maximum of absolute percentage deviations of the average rewards compared to the average rewards obtained by solving the evaluation equations with CPLEX

It can be seen that all solution procedures were implemented correctly as they gave nearly identical average rewards over all 100 problem instances. For simulation, the estimated average rewards of 99 problem instances staid within the maximum relative error γ of 0.5% while the estimated average reward for one problem instance differed by about 1% from the true average reward.

Table 3.2 gives the mean and standard deviations of the 100 running times for each solution procedure. It can be seen that some means differ greatly. In order to check if the differences in means have any statistical significance a statistical test has to be employed. In order to decide which statistical test should be used the data should be inspected and tested for normality first.

solution procedure	mean	standard deviation
evaluation equations (Gauss-Seidel)	1.6	1.6
evaluation equations (CPLEX)	26.2	30.7
stationary probabilities (Gauss-Seidel)	117.6	96.9
stationary probabilities (CPLEX)	193.3	48.5
simulation	11.8	7.8
value iteration	49.5	24.2

Table 3.2: Mean and standard deviation of running times in seconds

Thode (2002) recommends to graphically inspect the data by at least a histogram and a probability plot in order to identify distributional characteristics before employing a statistical test.

As the histograms and quantile-quantile (Q-Q) plots of the running times in figures 3.4 and 3.5 show, the running times do not seem to be normally distributed.

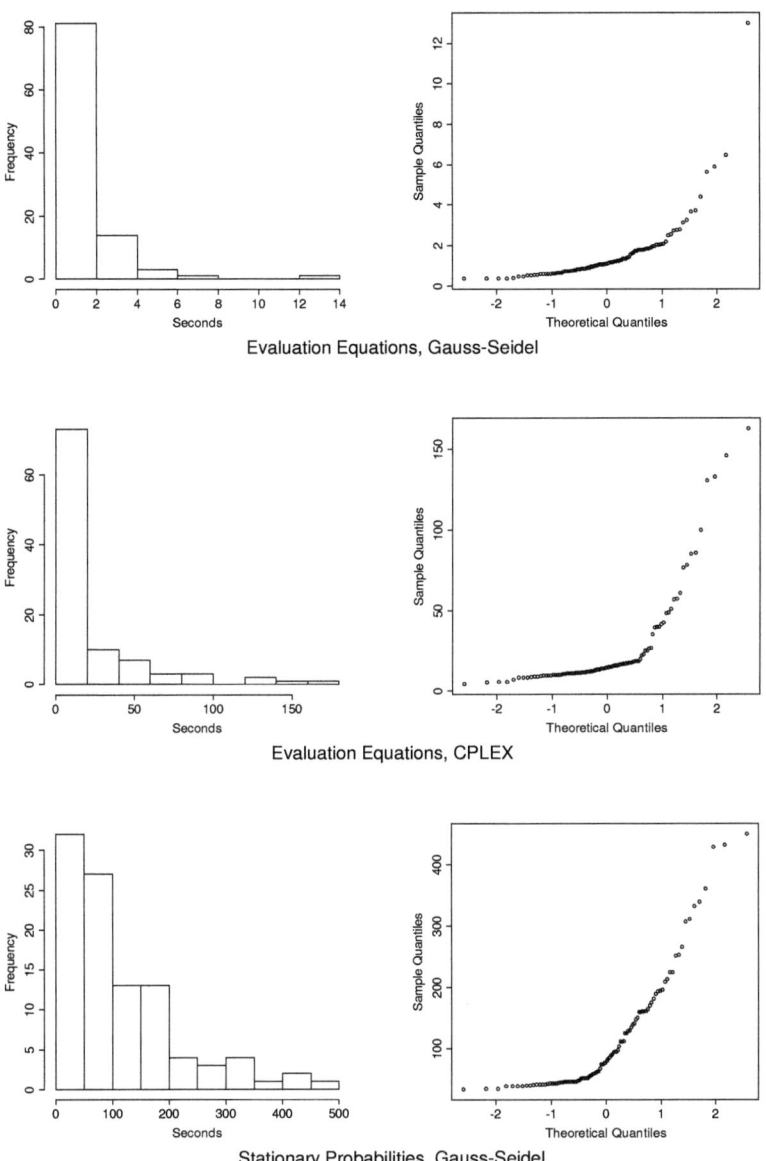

Figure 3.4: Histograms and Q-Q plots of 100 running times for solving the evaluation equations and for obtaining the stationary probabilities with the Gauss-Seidel procedure

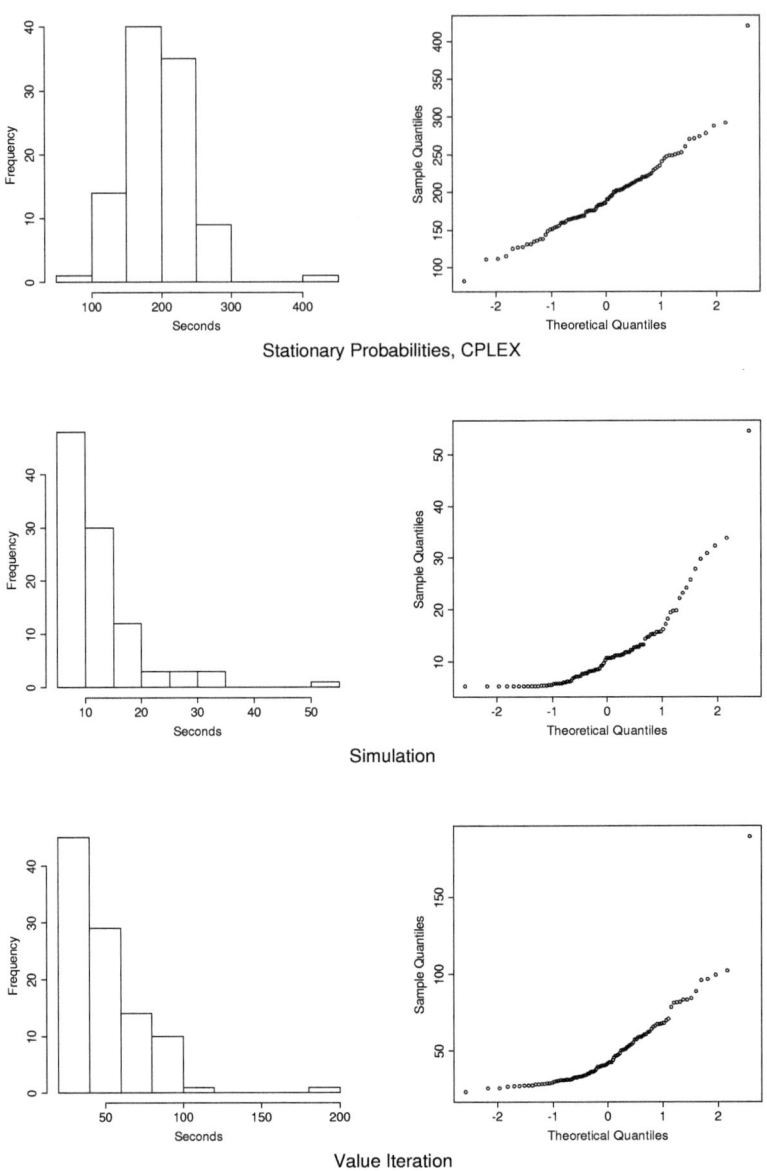

Figure 3.5: Histograms and Q-Q plots of 100 running times for obtaining the stationary probabilities with CPLEX, simulation and value iteration

As a statistical test for normality the Wilk-Shapiro test was chosen because it is recommended by both Thode (2002) and D'Agostino and Stephens (1986) as one of the most powerful tests for normality. The results of this test were obtained by the statistical computing system R, see R Development Core Team (2007), and are shown in table 3.3.

As table 3.3 shows, the p-value resulting from the Wilk-Shapiro test is significantly lower than the chosen significance level of 5% for all solution procedures. So, one can conclude that for every solution procedure the null hypothesis that the data are normally distributed can be rejected. Thus, a statistical test to compare the running times of the solution procedures which requires normally distributed data should not be used but rather a nonparametric test.

solution procedure	p-value
evaluation equations (Gauss-Seidel)	$2.754 \cdot 10^{-15}$
evaluation equations (CPLEX)	$5.644 \cdot 10^{-15}$
stationary probabilities (Gauss-Seidel)	$1.361 \cdot 10^{-10}$
stationary probabilities (CPLEX)	$5.521 \cdot 10^{-4}$
simulation	$1.704 \cdot 10^{-11}$
value iteration	$2.203 \cdot 10^{-10}$

Table 3.3: Wilk-Shapiro test for normality of the running times

As each of the 100 problem instances was used for all six solution procedures, the running times for the six solution procedures were not independent. From a statistical point of view, each problem instance can be viewed as a block while the solution procedures can be viewed as the treatments, see Conover (1999). Thus, a nonparametric test for a randomized complete block design and several dependent samples had to be used. Conover (1999) recommends two such tests for this situation, the Friedman test if there are more than five treatments and the Quade test if there are five or less treatments. As we considered six solution procedures, the Friedman test was applied with the statistics system R. The Friedman test gave a p-value of smaller than $2.2 \cdot 10^{-16}$, thus rejecting the null hypothesis that all solution procedures have equal running times.

In order to evaluate which solution procedures have higher running times than other solution procedures, multiple comparisons of the running times had to be performed. To carry out multiple comparisons, we adopted the procedure for multiple comparisons that is associated with the Friedman test, see Conover (1999). It turns out that at a significance level of 5%, the mean of the running times of every procedure was significantly different from the mean of the running times of each other procedure. Thus, the procedures could be ranked according to the means of the running times given in table 3.2. This ranking is shown in table 3.4. It follows that the solution of the evaluation equations with the Gauss-Seidel procedure was the fastest solution procedure for small problem instances.

solution procedure	rank
evaluation equations (Gauss-Seidel)	1
simulation	2
evaluation equations (CPLEX)	3
value iteration	4
stationary probabilities (Gauss-Seidel)	5
stationary probabilities (CPLEX)	6

Table 3.4: Ranking the solution procedures with regards to the running times for small problem instances

3.2.5.2   A Large Problem Instance

When looking at a large problem instance, a different picture emerges. We considered a problem instance with 1,000,000 states, 50 order classes and a traffic intensity of 1.5. For this problem instance, only the solution procedure of simulation was able to finish within a one hour time limit, taking 355 seconds. All five other solution procedures were not able to finish within the one hour time limit. This is due to higher memory requirements which are outlined in table 3.5. For the solution procedures with CPLEX only the memory requirements for generating the CPLEX problem file are given because the memory requirements of CPLEX itself are difficult to obtain.

It can be seen that the memory requirements depend on the number of states $|S|$ and on the number of order classes N of a given problem instance.

Solution Procedure	Memory Requirement in Bytes
Evaluation Equations (Gauss-Seidel)	$(16N + 61) \lvert S \rvert$
Evaluation Equations (CPLEX) (generating CPLEX file only)	$(4\,(N + 1 + S^{\mathrm{max}} + S_{D1}^{\mathrm{max}} + S_{D2}^{\mathrm{max}}) + 50)\,\lvert S \rvert$
Stationary Probabilities (Gauss-Seidel)	$(16N + 4\,(S^{\mathrm{max}} + S_{D1}^{\mathrm{max}} + S_{D2}^{\mathrm{max}}) + 76)\,\lvert S \rvert$
Stationary Probabilities (CPLEX) (generating CPLEX file only)	$(4\,(N + 1) + 8)\,\lvert S \rvert$
Simulation	$(4\,(N + 1) + 8)\,\lvert S \rvert$
Value Iteration	$(4\,(N + 1) + 32)\,\lvert S \rvert$

Table 3.5: Memory requirements for solution procedures

The memory requirements for the solution procedures "Evaluation Equations (CPLEX)" and "Stationary Probabilities (Gauss-Seidel)" are significantly higher than those of the other solution procedures because for these two solution procedures the set of source states that go into a given state under a certain policy has to be generated and stored while for the other four solution procedures only the set of target states that a given state can transition into has to be stored. The variable S_d^{max} is given by

$$S_d^{\mathrm{max}} = \max_{i \in S}\{S_d(i)\}$$

where $S_d(i)$ is the number of source states where decision d is taken and that go into state i. The variable S^{max} is given by $\max(S_{D1}^{\mathrm{max}}, S_{D2}^{\mathrm{max}})$.

It can be seen that simulation is one of the solution procedures with the lowest memory requirements. For two of the solution procedures, namely generating the CPLEX problem file for the solution procedure "Evaluation Equations (CPLEX)" on the one hand and "Stationary Probabilities (Gauss-Seidel)" on the other hand, the overall memory of the PC was not enough and the procedures terminated with an "out of memory" error. The three other solution procedures that could not finish within the one hour time limit were slowed down considerably because of an increased use of the swap file. For the case of obtaining the stationary probabilities with CPLEX, the CPLEX file could be generated but CPLEX itself could not finish within the one hour time limit.

One can conclude that for large problem instances, the average reward $g(\pi)$ of policy π can only be estimated by simulation.

3.3   Solving the Markov Decision Process

After a Markov decision process has been formulated, one wants to find an optimal policy π^{opt} which maximizes the average reward per period to obtain the optimal average reward $g(\pi^{\text{opt}})$. Different solution procedures for average reward unichain Markov decision processes exist, see e.g. Puterman (1994) or Tijms (1994). In the following, we describe the three most common algorithms for solving a Markov decision process.

3.3.1   Policy Iteration

One way to solve a unichain Markov decision process is given by the policy iteration algorithm. The policy iteration algorithm starts by choosing an arbitrary policy π_0. For the basic model of revenue management of this chapter a FCFS policy was chosen as the initial policy for the policy iteration algorithm. After the initial policy has been chosen, the algorithm evaluates the current policy by solving the evaluation equations (3.4). As we showed in the previous section, solving the evaluation equations by the Gauss-Seidel iterative method proved to be significantly faster than CPLEX, so the iterative method was chosen for this step of the policy iteration algorithm. After the average reward $g(\pi_n)$ and the relative values $v(i)$ have been calculated for the current policy π_n, a policy improvement step takes place in order to obtain policy π_{n+1}. If the policy improvement step does not alter the current policy, the policy iteration algorithm terminates. Otherwise, n is increased by one and the improved policy is evaluated. After the algorithm has terminated, the optimal policy π^{opt} is given by the last policy π_n and the optimal average reward $g(\pi^{\text{opt}})$ is given by the value of $g(\pi_n)$.

Algorithm 3.3 Policy iteration algorithm

$n \leftarrow 0$

choose an arbitrary starting policy π_0

repeat

    1. evaluate policy π_n by solving the evaluation equations

$$g(\pi_n) + v(i) - \sum_{j \in S} P^{\pi_n}(i,j)\, v(j) = R^{\pi_n}(i), \forall i \in S$$

    2. obtain the improved policy π_{n+1} by determining for each state $i \in S$ a decision d by

$$d = \arg\max_{d \in D(i)} \{R^d(i) + \sum_{j \in S} P^d(i,j)\, v(j)\}, \forall i \in S$$

    3. $n \leftarrow n + 1$

until $\pi_n = \pi_{n-1}$

$\pi^{\text{opt}} \leftarrow \pi_n$

$g(\pi^{\text{opt}}) \leftarrow g(\pi_n)$

3.3.2   Value Iteration

Another method to solve a Markov decision process is the value iteration algorithm which is shown in algorithm 3.4. The differences $\Delta V(i)$ of the values $V_n(i) - V_{n-1}(i)$ converge to an ϵ-optimal average reward which means that the average reward found by the value iteration algorithm will differ at most by $100\epsilon\%$ from the true optimal average reward.

Each value V_n during every iteration n is calculated by finding the decision d in every state i that maximizes V_n. The ϵ-optimal policy is determined by using the decisions d for every state i after $\underline{\Delta V}$ and $\overline{\Delta V}$ have converged within $\epsilon\%$ of $\overline{\Delta V}$. The convergence parameter ϵ was set to 0.5%.

3.3.3   Linear Programming

A third solution procedure to obtain the optimal policy π^{opt} for a unichain Markov decision process is given by solving the following linear program.

$$\text{Maximize} \quad g(\pi^{\mathrm{opt}}) = \sum_{i\in S} \sum_{d\in D(i)} R^d(i)\, \tilde{P}^d(i) \tag{3.10}$$

subject to

$$\sum_{d\in D(j)} \tilde{P}^d(j) = \sum_{i\in S} \sum_{d\in D(i)} P^d(i,j)\, \tilde{P}^d(i), \forall j \in S$$

$$\sum_{i\in S} \sum_{d\in D(i)} \tilde{P}^d(i) = 1$$

$$\tilde{P}^d(i) \geq 0, \forall i \in S, \forall d \in D(i)$$

The optimal policy π^{opt} is obtained by choosing each $d \in D(i)$ in each state i to be the decision d for which the stationary probability $\tilde{P}^d(i) > 0$. The optimal average reward $g(\pi^{\mathrm{opt}})$ is given by the value of the objective function (3.10) after the linear program has been solved.

Algorithm 3.4 Value iteration algorithm

$n \leftarrow 1$

$V_0(i) \leftarrow 0, \forall i \in S$

repeat

    1. compute for every state $i \in S$ the values $V_n(i)$ by

$$V_n(i) \leftarrow \max_{d \in D(i)} \{R^d(i) + \sum_{j \in S} P^d(i,j)V_{n-1}(j)\}, \forall i \in S$$

    2. compute the bounds

$$\underline{\Delta V} \leftarrow \min_{i \in S}\{V_n(i) - V_{n-1}(i)\} \text{ and } \overline{\Delta V} \leftarrow \max_{i \in S}\{V_n(i) - V_{n-1}(i)\}$$

    3. $n \leftarrow n + 1$

until $\overline{\Delta V} - \underline{\Delta V} \leq \epsilon \underline{\Delta V}$

obtain the ϵ-optimal policy π^ϵ by choosing the decision d for each state i by

$$d \leftarrow \arg \max_{d \in D(i)} \{R^d(i) + \sum_{j \in S} P^d(i,j)V_{n-1}(j)\}$$

obtain an estimate $\widehat{g}(\pi^\epsilon)$ for the average reward of the ϵ-optimal policy by

$$\widehat{g}(\pi^\epsilon) \leftarrow \underline{\Delta V} + 0.5 \left(\overline{\Delta V} - \underline{\Delta V}\right)$$

3.3.4   Comparing Solution Procedures

In this section we will compare the three solution procedures with regards to their running times.

3.3.4.1   Small Problem Instances

The same 100 problem instances with $|S| = 10{,}000$ states that were used to compare the solution procedures to evaluate a given policy were used to compare the solution procedures to solve the Markov decision process. In order to check if all solution procedures obtained the same optimal average reward, the maximum of the absolute percentage deviations of the average reward that was obtained by solving the linear program was compared to the two other solution procedures. The results are depicted in table 3.6. It can be seen that all three solution procedures obtain almost identical optimal average rewards $g(\pi^{\mathrm{opt}})$ and were thus correctly implemented.

Solution procedure	Mean	Maximum
Policy iteration	0.00%	0.00%
Value iteration	0.09%	0.23%

Table 3.6: Mean and maximum of absolute percentage deviations of the average rewards obtained by two solution procedures compared to the average rewards obtained by solving the linear program with CPLEX

Solution procedure	Mean	Standard deviation
Policy iteration	4.2	4.3
Value iteration	58.9	29.5
Linear programming	365.8	142.3

Table 3.7: Mean and standard deviation of running times

Table 3.7 shows the mean and standard deviation of the running times for each solution procedure after solving the 100 problem instances.

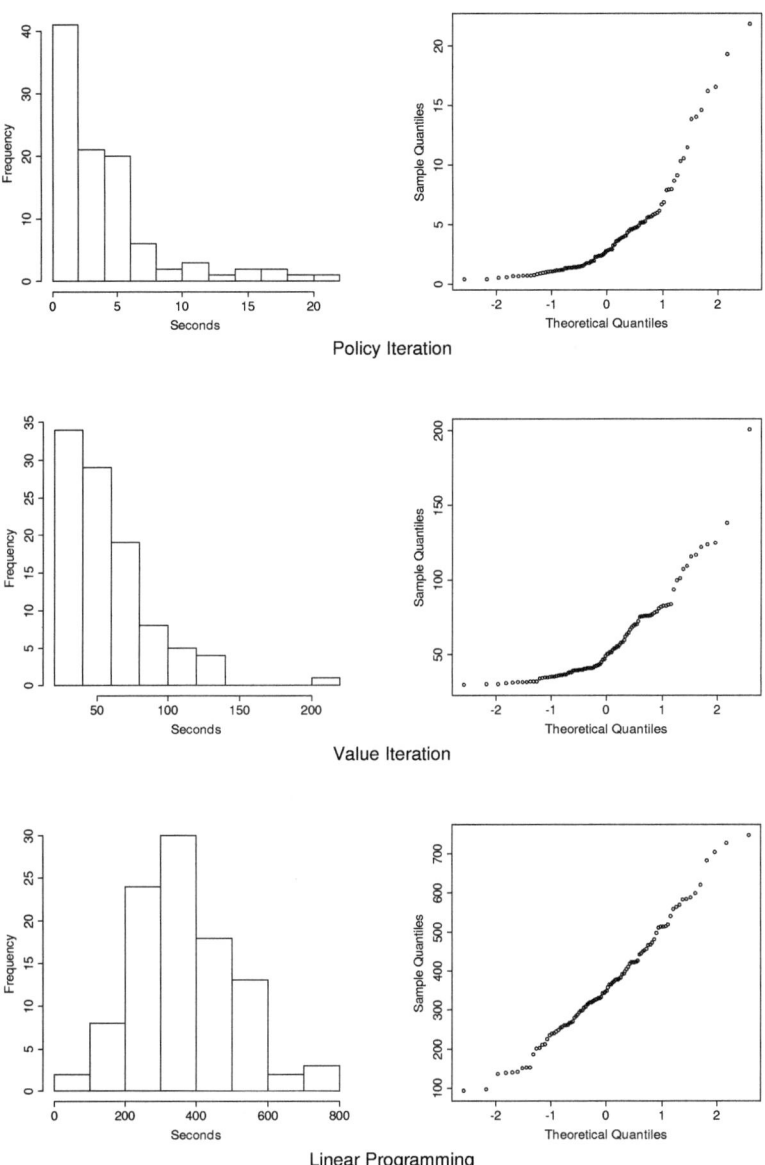

Figure 3.6: Histograms and Q-Q plots of 100 running times for obtaining the optimal policy

Policy iteration seems to dominate the other solution procedures, but in order to see if this assumption can be substantiated, a statistical test has to be employed.

The statistical design can be viewed as a randomized complete block design with several dependent samples. In order to decide what type of statistical test should be employed, the data of the running times have to be inspected and tested for normality first. Figure 3.6 shows the histograms and Q-Q plots for the running time data.

Only the running times of linear programming seem to be somewhat normally distributed while the running times of the other solution procedures seem to be highly nonnormal. This is confirmed by the Wilk-Shapiro test whose p-values can be seen in table 3.8.

Solution procedure	p-value
Policy iteration	$2.338 \cdot 10^{-11}$
Value iteration	$1.562 \cdot 10^{-9}$
Linear programming	0.118

Table 3.8: Wilk-Shapiro test for normality of the running times

As the running time data of two solution procedure are not normally distributed, a nonparametric test has to be employed. Conover (1999) recommends using the Quade test as there are only three treatments involved. Using the statistical system R, a p-value of $2.2 \cdot 10^{-16}$ strongly suggests that the null hypothesis that the running times of all solution procedures are equal can be rejected. Performing the multiple comparisons procedure recommended by Conover (1999), it turns out that the running times of each solution procedure are significantly different from the running times of the other two solution procedures. Thus, the solution procedures can be ranked according to their mean running times which are shown in table 3.7. One can conclude that the policy iteration algorithm is superior for small problem instances.

3.3.4.2   A Large Problem Instance

The same large problem instance that was used for analyzing the procedures to evaluate the average reward of a given policy in section 3.2.5.2 was applied to the three solution procedures that solve the Markov decision process. It turns out that neither solution procedure can solve this problem instance within a one hour time limit. This result shows the need for a heuristic procedure.

3.4 A Heuristic Procedure

When comparing a FCFS policy which accepts all orders if the current capacity situation allows it to the optimal policy π^{opt} which can be obtained by one of the solution procedures of the previous section, one notices that the optimal policy differs from the FCFS policy by rejecting unprofitable order classes to a certain extent. Thus, the idea for the heuristic procedure is to reject orders from unprofitable order classes while accepting orders from order classes with a higher profit margin. The profitability of an order class $n \in \{1, \cdots, N\}$ will not be measured by its profit margin m_n, but rather by its relative profit margin m_n/u_n, i.e. m_n divided by the capacity usage u_n. The relative profit margin is an indicator of how profitable it is to allocate the machine for one period to an order of class n. The relative profit margin for the dummy order class 0 is set to 0. Before the heuristic can start, the order classes are sorted ascendingly by their relative profit margins.

Figure 3.7 shows how a good heuristic policy might look like for five hypothetical order classes which have been sorted in ascending order by their relative profit margins, $m_n/u_n \le m_{n+1}/u_{n+1}, n \in \{1, 2, \ldots, N-1\}$. For each order class the policy specifies if and under which circumstances this order class is rejected or not.

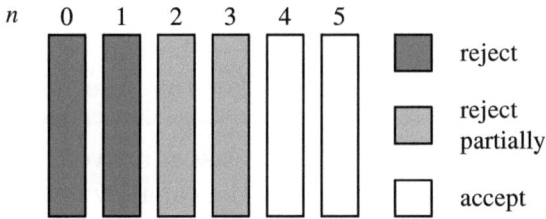

Figure 3.7: Accepting and rejecting order classes

The dummy order class 0, which represents the case that no order arrives in a given period is always set to rejection. The exemplary policy in figure 3.7

rejects order class 1, the order class with the lowest relative profit margin, in all system states even if it could be accepted in some system states. This rejection of order class 1 might increase the average reward of the company in order to reserve capacity for order classes with higher profit margins. Order classes 2 and 3 are only partially rejected which means that they are accepted in some system states but rejected in all other system states, even if they could be accepted in some of those other system states. Order classes 4 and 5 which have the highest relative profit margins are accepted in all system states where acceptance is possible. The optimal policy will be the optimal combination of which order classes are completely rejected, which order classes are partially rejected and which order classes are fully accepted.

In order to develop a heuristic procedure it is useful to represent each policy of mapping a decision $d \in D[(n, c)]$ to each state (n, c) by an N-dimensional vector $\theta^T = (\tau_0, \tau_1, \ldots, \tau_N)$. The threshold τ_n specifies for which capacity usages c an order of class n should be accepted or rejected. If $c < \tau_n$, the order should be accepted, while if $c \geq \tau_n$ the order should be rejected, see figure 3.8.

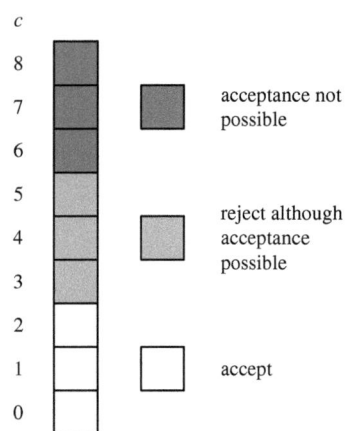

Figure 3.8 shows an order class n with $l_n - u_n + 1 = 6$ and a policy for this order class that is described by $\tau_n = 3$. The term $l_n - u_n + 1$ represents the minimum capacity usage c where orders of class n can not be accepted any more. This is due to the fact that orders can only be accepted if $c + u_n \leq l_n$ which can be converted to $c \leq l_n - u_n$. For the order class n in figure 3.8, $l_n - u_n + 1 = 6$ and thus if an order of class n arrives at the company and the capacity is booked out for more than 6 periods, orders of that order class have to be rejected because the company cannot meet the lead time l_n that the customers of order class

Figure 3.8: Partial rejection of order class $n, l_n - u_n + 1 = 6, \tau_n = 3$

n demand. The partial rejection of order class n in figure 3.8 is depicted by the fact that $\tau_n = 3$. This means that orders could be accepted up to a capacity booking level c of 6 units, but incoming orders of this class are rejected for any $c \geq 3$. This partial rejection of order class n might be more profitable for the company than to either completely accept it because of a high relative profit margin m_n/u_n or to completely reject it because of a rather low relative profit margin. If τ_n is set to $l_n - u_n + 1$ it means that all incoming orders of class n are rejected. If τ_n is set to 0 it means that all orders of class n are accepted as long as the capacity booking level c is below $l_n - u_n + 1$.

Denote now by π the policy that the order classes $n \in \{0, \dots, \pi\}$ are completely rejected and the order classes $n \in \{\pi + 1, \dots, N\}$ are completely accepted. The idea of the heuristic is to evaluate various policies and find good policies by simulation comparisons. Each policy π results in a Markov reward process with an associated average reward per period $g(\pi)$ whose estimate $\widehat{g}(\pi)$ can be obtained by simulation. The heuristic starts by comparing policies $\pi = 0$ and $\pi = 1$ by simulation which is shown in figure 3.9. In order to simplify the display, $l_n - u_n + 1$ is set to be constant for all order classes n which is usually not the case.

If $\widehat{g}(0) > \widehat{g}(1)$ policy 0 of accepting all order classes is accepted as the optimal policy and the heuristic stops. Otherwise, $\pi \leftarrow \pi + 1$ and the procedure continues likewise until $\widehat{g}(\pi) > \widehat{g}(\pi + 1)$. At that point, policy π has the highest average reward of all policies compared so far, for an example see figure 3.10 where $\pi = 2$.

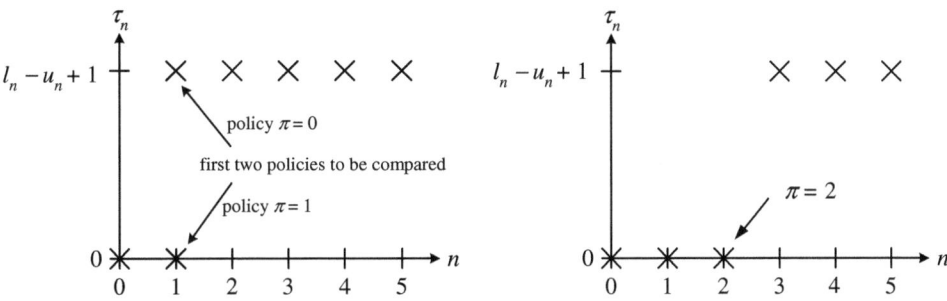

Figure 3.9: Comparing policies   Figure 3.10: Policy $\pi = 2$

Now, the heuristic tries to further optimize policy π by comparing it to policy π^+ which is obtained by setting

$$\tau_{\pi+1} \leftarrow \lfloor \frac{l_{\pi+1} - u_{\pi+1} + 1}{2} \rfloor$$

see figure 3.11. If $\widehat{g}(\pi^+) > \widehat{g}(\pi)$ policy π^+ is accepted to be the best policy $\tilde{\pi}$ found by the heuristic. Otherwise, policy π is compared to policy π^- which is obtained by setting

$$\tau_\pi \leftarrow \lfloor \frac{l_\pi - u_\pi + 1}{2} \rfloor.$$

If $\widehat{g}(\pi^-) > \widehat{g}(\pi)$ policy π^- is accepted to be the best policy $\tilde{\pi}$ found by the heuristic, otherwise $\tilde{\pi}$ results from policy π.

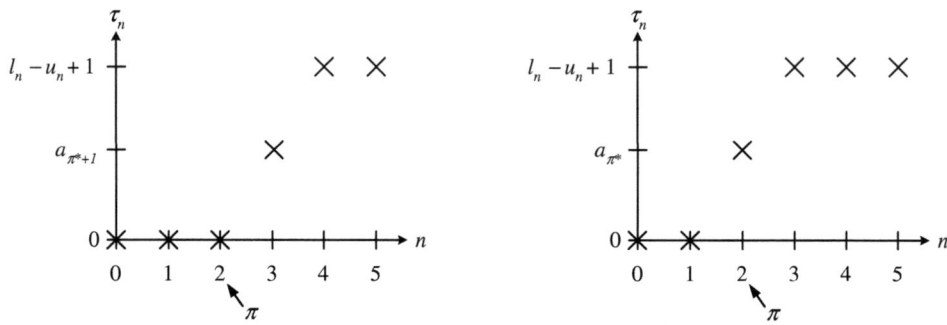

Figure 3.11: Policies π^+ and π^-

Two policies are compared following the paired-t confidence interval approach, see Law and Kelton (2000). This approach defines the random variable $Z_i = X_{1i} - X_{2i}$ where X_{1i} and X_{2i} are the average rewards obtained from replication i under the two policies that are being compared. An unbiased estimator for the variance of $\overline{Z}(n) = 1/n \sum_{i=1}^{n} Z_i$ after n replications is given by

$$\widehat{\text{Var}}[\overline{Z}(n)] = \frac{\sum_{i=1}^{n}[Z_i - \overline{Z}(n)]^2}{n(n-1)}$$

In order to reduce the estimated variance $\widehat{\text{Var}}[\overline{Z}(n)]$ and thus to speed up the simulation comparison, common random numbers are used when two policies are compared. Common random numbers in this case mean that the order arrival pattern during a replication is identical for both policies.

A policy is determined to outperform another policy and the sequential simulation comparison is thus stopped after n replications if the following criterion is fulfilled:

$$|\overline{Z}(n)| - t_{n-1,1-\alpha/2}\sqrt{\widehat{\text{Var}[\overline{Z}(n)]}} > 0$$

where $t_{n-1,1-\alpha/2}\sqrt{\widehat{\text{Var}[\overline{Z}(n)]}}$ is the half-width of the $100(1-\alpha)$ percent confidence interval for the true difference of the two average rewards being compared.

If two average rewards to be compared are very close, no significant difference between the two policies can be detected within a reasonable amount of replications. For this case the stopping criterion to end the comparison is:

$$|\overline{Z}(n)| + t_{n-1,1-\alpha/2}\sqrt{\widehat{\text{Var}[\overline{Z}(n)]}} < 0.5\% \cdot \min\{\overline{X}_1(n), \overline{X}_2(n)\}$$

Here the simulation comparison stops if the policies do not differ significantly by more than half a percent. In this case, the policy which accepts more orders overall is set to dominate the policy it was compared to.

After $\tilde{\pi}$, the best policy found by the heuristic procedure, has been determined, the corresponding average reward $g(\tilde{\pi})$ is estimated by simulation with a maximum relative error γ of 0.5%. As $g(\tilde{\pi})$ has to be estimated more accurately than the individual average rewards of two policies that are being compared, the replication lengths for the simulation runs of policy comparisons can be set less conservatively than the replication lengths for estimating $g(\tilde{\pi})$. This is illustrated in figure 3.12 for a problem instance with 10,000 states, 5 order classes and a traffic intensity of 1. The replication length is set to 200,000 periods when comparing policies and to 600,000 periods when the average reward of the best policy found is estimated. The warmup period of 10,000 periods is left equal for both purposes.

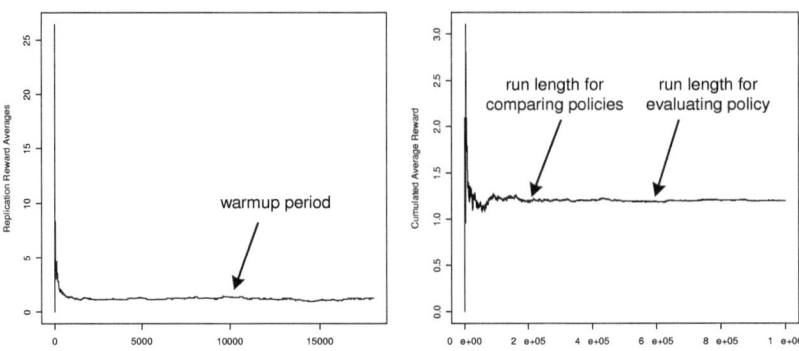

Figure 3.12: Different run lengths for comparing and evaluating policies

3.5   Numerical Results

3.5.1   Comparing the Optimal Policy to a FCFS Policy

It is of interest to evaluate what benefits can be realized by using an optimal policy and thus applying revenue management instead of using a FCFS policy which accepts all orders whenever possible. Thus the two policies were compared with regards to the average reward per period for three problem classes which are outlined in table 3.9.

problem class $\rightarrow$	1	2	3
number of states	10,000	50,000	100,000
number of order classes	[5, 20]	[5, 30]	[5, 50]
traffic intensity	[1, 2.5]	[1, 2.5]	[1, 2.5]
maximum lead time	[476, 1667]	[1613, 8333]	[1961, 16667]

Table 3.9: Problem classes for comparing the optimal policy to a FCFS policy

All problem instances that were created within a certain problem class had the same number of states as given in table 3.9. The number of order classes for a certain problem instance was drawn from a certain uniform distribution for each problem class. The maximum lead time, l^{max}, was calculated by equation (3.2) and varied between the two values that are given in table 3.9, depending on the number of order classes that had been drawn for a certain problem instance.

The average rewards of the FCFS and optimal policies were obtained by policy iteration. The results of comparing the optimal policy to a FCFS policy are shown in table 3.10.

problem class $\rightarrow$	1	2	3
problem instances	1,000	1,000	200
average [%]	2.5	2.3	2.1
minimum [%]	0.0	0.0	0.0
maximum [%]	41.2	34.0	32.8
standard deviation [%]	4.5	3.7	3.8
average running time [sec.]	3.1	29.4	87.5

Table 3.10: Percentage deviations $\Delta^{\mathrm{FCFS-opt}}$ of average rewards of the optimal policy compared to the FCFS policy

As the average running times of computing the average rewards are low for small problem instances, 1,000 problem instances were created for problem classes 1 and 2. As the running times for problem class 3 increased considerably, 200 problem instances were created for this problem class.

Table 3.10 shows the average, minimum, maximum and standard deviation for the percentage deviations $\Delta^{\mathrm{FCFS-opt}}$ of the average reward per period of the optimal policy compared to the FCFS policy. The percentage deviation $\Delta^{\mathrm{FCFS-opt}}$ of a certain problem instance within a problem class was calculated by

$$\Delta^{\mathrm{FCFS-opt}} = \frac{g(\pi^{\mathrm{opt}}) - g(\pi^{\mathrm{FCFS}})}{g(\pi^{\mathrm{FCFS}})} \cdot 100\%$$

where $g(\pi^{\mathrm{opt}})$ and $g(\pi^{\mathrm{FCFS}})$ were the average rewards per period of the optimal and the FCFS policies, respectively.

Table 3.10 shows that the optimal policy outperforms the FCFS policy by between 2.1% and 2.5% on average although there are problem instances where applying revenue management instead of using a FCFS policy increases the average reward per period by as much as 41%.

Figure 3.13 shows that most percentage deviations lie in the $[0, 5]\%$ interval but that some observations lie in higher intervals. Two of the factors which might have an influence on the percentage deviations of the average rewards of the optimal policy compared to the FCFS policy are examined subsequently. These factors are the traffic intensity and the tightness of lead times.

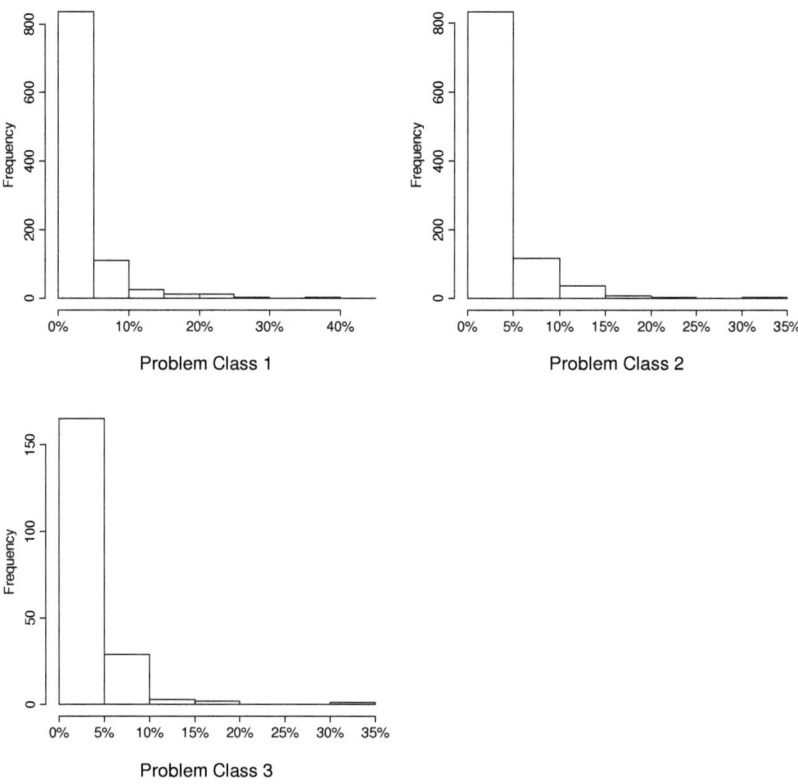

Figure 3.13: Histograms of the percentage deviations $\Delta^{\text{FCFS}-\text{opt}}$ of the optimal policy compared to the FCFS policy

3.5.1.1 Influence of the Traffic Intensity

The first factor to be evaluated is the traffic intensity which is given by $\rho = \sum_{n=1}^{N} p_n u_n$ for a certain problem instance. Kniker and Burman (2001) show for a single problem instance that the average reward increases with an increase in the traffic intensity. In order to explore if this relationship holds true generally, problem instances were created for the problem classes that were defined above, see table 3.9. The problem instances were created in two sets for each problem class. In the first set, each problem instance has a traffic intensity of 1 and in the second set, each problem instance has a traffic intensity of 2.5. For example, for problem class 1, 1,000 problem instances were created with a traffic intensity of 1 and 1,000 problem instances were created with a traffic intensity of 2.5. For each set the percentage deviations of the optimal policy compared to the FCFS were computed. The results can be seen in table 3.11.

problem class $\rightarrow$		1	2	3
problem instances	($\rho = 1/\rho = 2.5$)	1000/1000	1000/1000	200/200
average [%]	($\rho = 1/\rho = 2.5$)	0.1/5.8	0.1/5.5	0.1/5.5
minimum [%]	($\rho = 1/\rho = 2.5$)	0.0/0.0	0.0/0.0	0.0/0.0
maximum [%]	($\rho = 1/\rho = 2.5$)	4.0/55.3	1.9/85.0	1.7/44.3
std. dev. [%]	($\rho = 1/\rho = 2.5$)	0.4/6.7	0.2/6.3	0.2/6.2

Table 3.11: $\Delta^{\mathrm{FCFS-opt}}$ with different traffic intensities

Table 3.11 shows that $\Delta^{\mathrm{FCFS-opt}}$ seems to depend on the traffic intensity. For a relatively low traffic intensity of 1, the average percentage deviations are 0.1% while for a higher traffic intensity of 2.5, the average percentage deviations range from 5.5% to 5.8%.

In order to test this apparent dependency on the traffic intensity for statistical significance the data has to be analyzed for normality so an adequate statistical test can be chosen. As figures 3.14 and 3.15 show, the percentage deviations do not seem to be distributed normally.

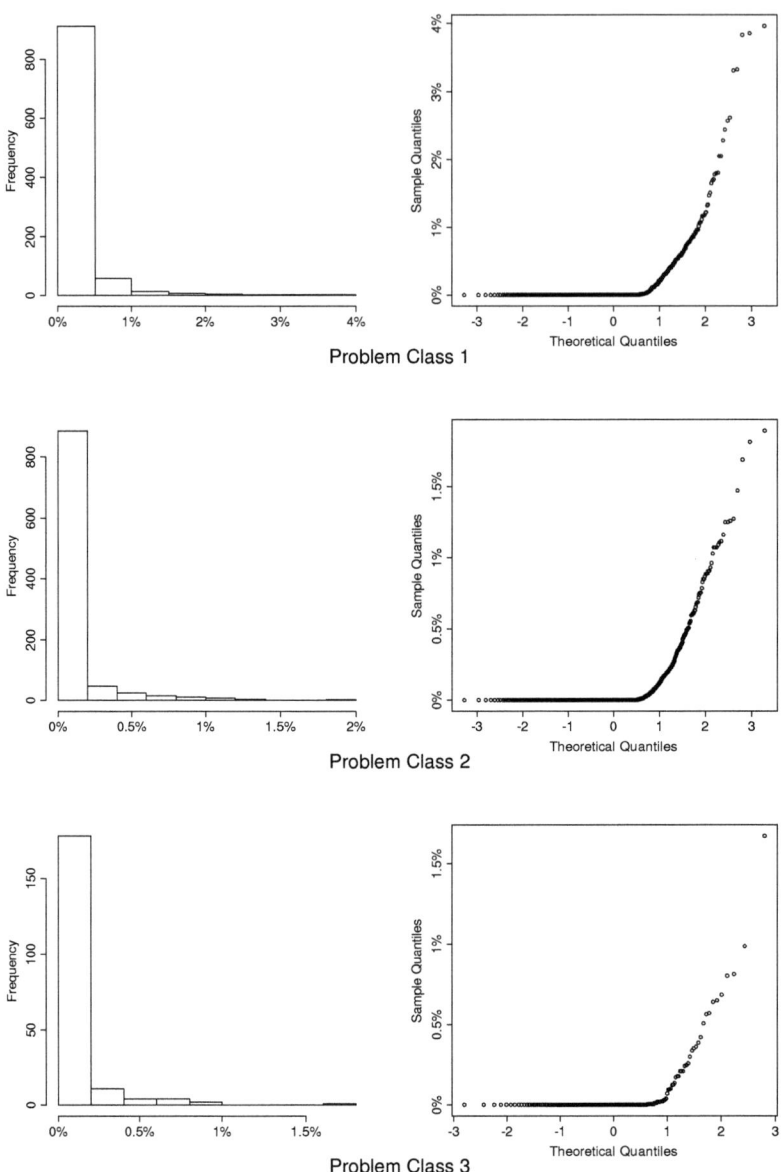

Figure 3.14: Histograms and Q-Q-plots of $\Delta^{\mathrm{FCFS-opt}}$ with a traffic intensity of $\rho = 1$

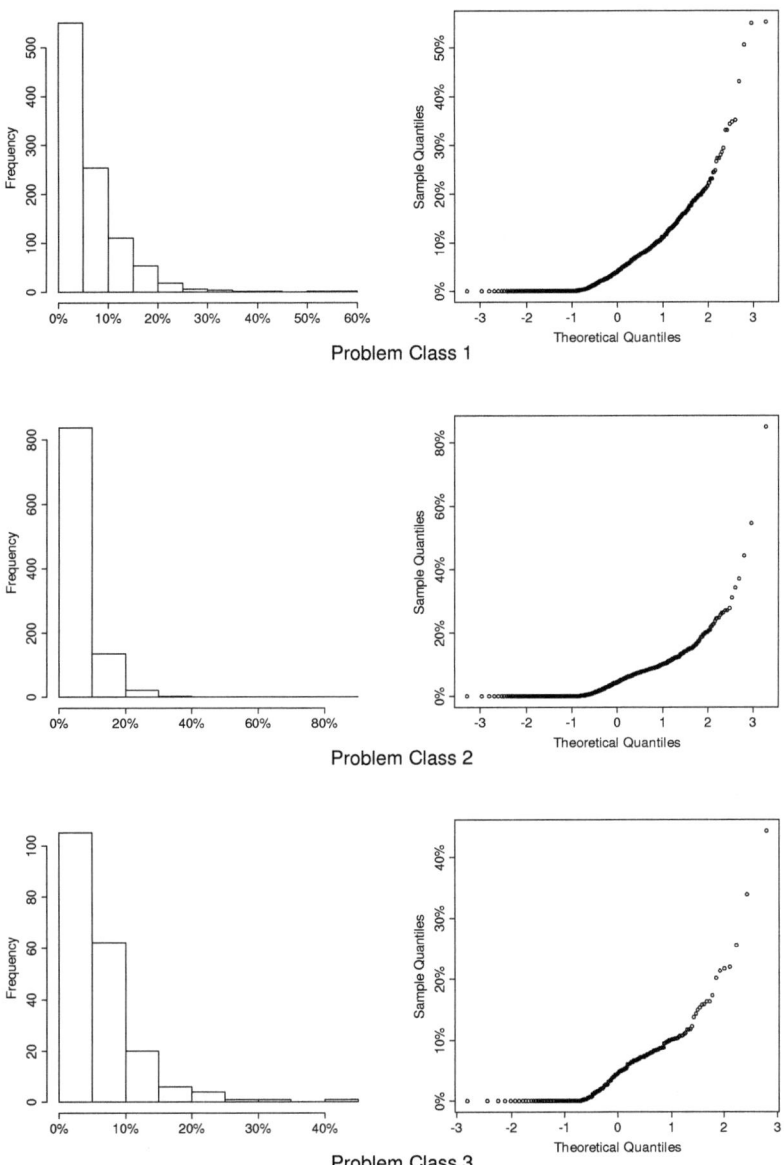

Figure 3.15: Histograms and Q-Q-plots of $\Delta^{\text{FCFS}-\text{opt}}$ with a traffic intensity of $\rho = 2.5$

This is confirmed by the Wilk-Shapiro test which gives a p-value smaller than 10^{-15} for the two scenarios and for all 3 problem classes. As the data are not normally distributed, a nonparametric test procedure has to be used. As there are two independent samples that are compared within each problem class, the Mann-Whitney test is used, see Conover (1999). An upper-tailed version of this test is used to test the null hypothesis

$$H_0 : F(x) = G(x)$$

versus the alternative hypothesis

$$H_1 : F(x) < G(x)$$

where $F(x)$ and $G(x)$ are the distribution functions corresponding to the percentage deviations of having a traffic intensity of 1 and 2.5, respectively. The results of the Mann-Whitney test confirm the impression that the traffic intensity has an influence on the value of revenue management. Using the statistical computing system R, in all three problem classes a p-value which is smaller than 10^{-16} is obtained. This suggests with near certainty that problem instances with a traffic intensity of 2.5 have a larger distribution function than problem instances with a traffic intensity of 1, confirming the preliminary result in Kniker and Burman (2001).

3.5.1.2   Influence of the Tightness of Lead Times

Another factor that can be explored is the tightness of lead times. Kniker and Burman (2001) hypothesize that if lead times are tight, the average reward obtained by the FCFS policy should not differ much from the average reward obtained by using revenue management. We now show that this statement is only true if lead times are short and that for tight, but longer lead times revenue management still provides a certain benefit.

We tested the influence of the tightness of lead times on the percentage deviation of the average reward of the optimal policy compared to the average reward of the FCFS policy. In order to test the hypothesis that tighter lead times lead to a decrease of the average percentage deviation of the average rewards, 1,000 problem instances were created for problem classes 1 and 2 and 200 problem instances were created for problem class 3. In each problem instance the lead time of each order class was set equal to the capacity usage of the order class, thus creating very tight lead times. The traffic intensity of each of these problem instances was set to 2.5 because with low traffic intensities, the percentage deviations are usually near zero, see the previous section.

The percentage deviations of the average rewards of the optimal policy compared to the FCFS policy of these problem instances were compared to the percentage deviations of the problem instances with a traffic intensity of 2.5 that were used in the previous section 3.5.1.1, which had lead times that vary between the order class usage u_n of the order class of a certain problem instance and the maximum lead time $l^{\max}$ of that problem instance. The results of comparing the percentage deviations of the average rewards of problem instances with tight lead times with problem instances with normal lead times can be seen in table 3.12.

problem class →		1	2	3
problem instances	(tight/normal)	1000/1000	1000/1000	200/200
average [%]	(tight/normal)	4.0/5.8	4.0/5.5	4.6/5.5
minimum [%]	(tight/normal)	0.0/0.0	0.0/0.0	0.0/0.0
maximum [%]	(tight/normal)	20.4/55.3	19.6/85.0	16.6/44.3
std. dev. [%]	(tight/normal)	4.1/6.7	4.0/6.3	4.1/6.2

Table 3.12: $\Delta^{\text{FCFS}-\text{opt}}$ for tight and normal lead times

Table 3.12 seems to suggest that problem instances with tighter lead times do not have as great a potential for using revenue management as problem instances where lead times are not tight. In order to test this hypothesis statistically, the data were tested for normality. Figure 3.16 shows the histograms and Q-Q-plots of the percentage deviations of comparing the optimal policy to a FCFS policy with tight lead times.

They do not seem to be distributed normally which is confirmed by the Wilk-Shapiro test. Table 3.13 shows that the null hypothesis that the data are normally distributed can be rejected for all three problem classes. Thus, a nonparametric test has to be used for two independent samples and the Mann-Whitney test is employed again.

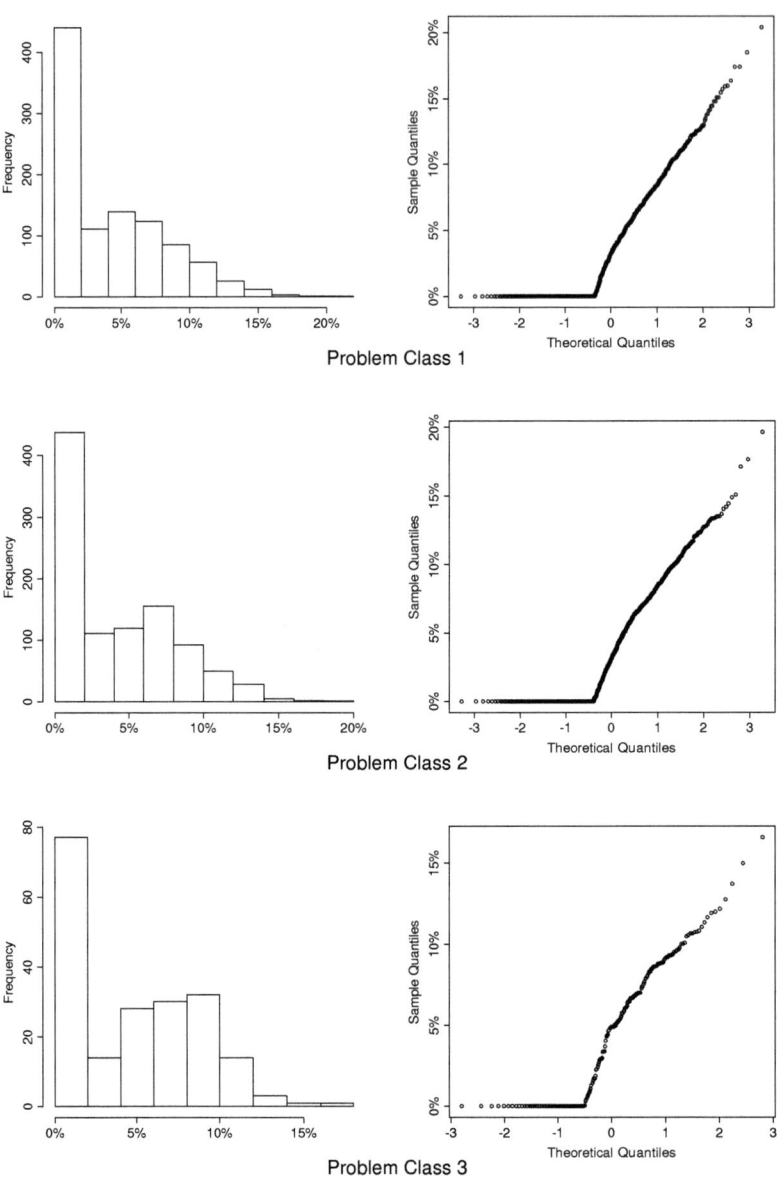

Figure 3.16: Histograms and Q-Q-plots of $\Delta^{\text{FCFS}-\text{opt}}$ with tight lead times and a traffic intensity of $\rho = 2.5$

Problem Class	1	2	3
p-value	$< 2.2 \cdot 10^{-16}$	$< 2.2 \cdot 10^{-16}$	$1.061 \cdot 10^{-10}$

Table 3.13: Wilk-Shapiro test for normality

Problem Class	1	2	3
p-value	$1.05 \cdot 10^{-13}$	$2.374 \cdot 10^{-12}$	0.119

Table 3.14: Mann-Whitney test

The Mann-Whitney test shows that for problem classes 1 and 2 the alternative hypothesis that the percentage deviations with tight lead times tend to be lower than the percentage deviations with normal lead times can be accepted, see table 3.14. For problem class 3, the null hypothesis that the distribution functions of the percentage deviations are equal can not be rejected at a significance level of 0.05. Thus, for problem class 3 the result is that the tightness of lead times does not have a significant influence on the potential of revenue management although the average $\Delta^{\text{FCFS}-\text{opt}}$ of 4.6 for tight lead times is lower than the average $\Delta^{\text{FCFS}-\text{opt}}$ of 5.5 for normal lead times.

This different result for problem class 3 may be due to the lower number of 200 observations versus 1,000 observations for problem classes 1 and 2 which might be too few observations to detect any significant difference in the percentage deviations $\Delta^{\text{FCFS}-\text{opt}}$ for problem class 3. As we have shown for problem classes 1 and 2, though, one can conclude that tight lead times decrease the potential of using revenue management compared to a FCFS policy.

In contrast to the hypothesis by Kniker and Burman (2001) that the percentage deviation of the average reward of the optimal policy compared to the average reward of the FCFS policy should be near zero when lead times are tight, we found that the percentage deviation averaged around 4%, see table 3.12. This means that even if lead times are tight, revenue management still has an advantage over a FCFS policy. This positive percentage deviation can be explained by the fact that even if the lead times in our numerical tests are tight, they are not as short as in the example by Kniker and Burman

(2001). Thus, by accepting a relatively unprofitable order with a tight, but relatively long lead time under a FCFS policy, the company is binding its capacity for this relatively long lead time and thus has to refuse more profitable orders that arrive in the mean time. It follows that revenue management has a positive impact if tight lead times are not too short, but that the optimal average reward nears the average reward obtained by a FCFS policy if tight lead times are also short.

3.5.2   Comparing the Heuristic to an Optimal Procedure

In order to assess how well the heuristic procedure performs it was compared to the policy iteration algorithm. The problem classes used to perform the comparison were the same as in section 3.5.1, see table 3.9. The results of comparing the heuristic procedure to the optimal procedure can be seen in table 3.15.

problem class $\rightarrow$	1	2	3
problem instances	500	500	200
average [%]	0.3	0.3	0.3
minimum [%]	0.0	0.0	0.0
maximum [%]	4.4	5.0	3.3
standard deviation [%]	0.6	0.5	0.5
running time heuristic [sec.]	28.7	119.0	249.2
running time policy iteration [sec.]	3.1	29.4	87.5

Table 3.15: Percentage deviations Δ^{H-opt} of average rewards obtained by the heuristic policy compared to the average rewards obtained by the optimal policy

Because the heuristic procedure had higher running times, only the first 500 scenarios were used for problem classes 1 and 2 while all 200 scenarios were used for problem class 3. The percentage deviation of the average reward obtained by the heuristic procedure was compared to the average reward obtained by the optimal procedure for each problem instance. This percentage deviation Δ^{H-opt} of a certain problem instance was calculated by

$$\Delta^{\text{H}-\text{opt}} = \frac{g(\pi^{\text{opt}}) - g(\tilde{\pi})}{g(\tilde{\pi})} \cdot 100\%$$

where $g(\pi^{\text{opt}})$ and $g(\tilde{\pi})$ were the average reward per period of the optimal and the heuristic procedure, respectively.

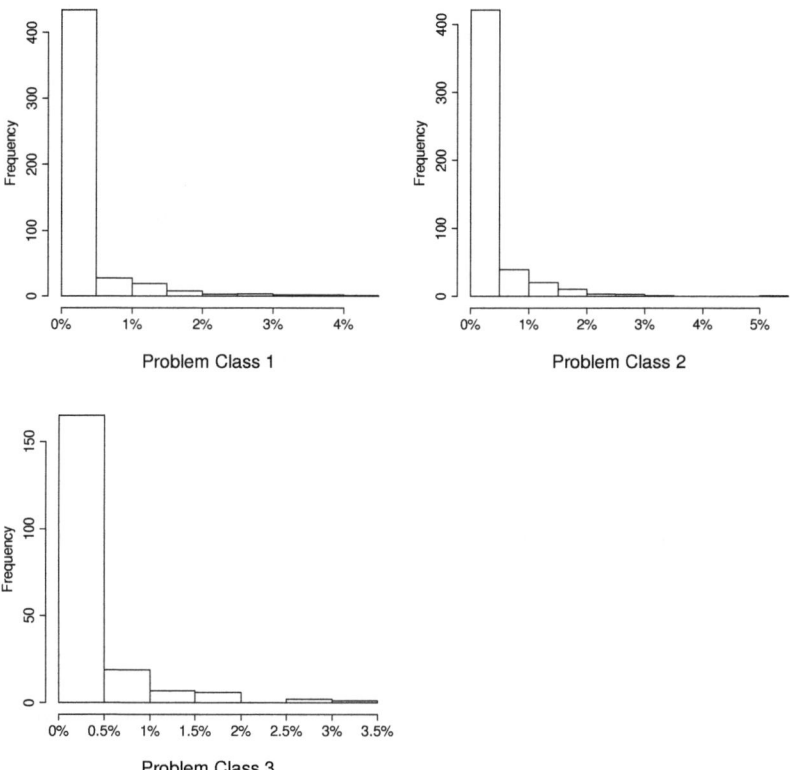

Figure 3.17: Histograms of the percentage deviations $\Delta^{\text{H}-\text{opt}}$ of average rewards when comparing the optimal procedure to the heuristic procedure

Table 3.15 shows that the heuristic procedure performs 0.3% worse on average than the optimal procedure for all three problem classes. The worst cases for the three problem classes were deviations of 4.4%, 5.0% and 3.3%.

Figure 3.17 shows that in most problem instances, the average reward obtained by the heuristic procedure differed between 0% and 0.5% from the average reward obtained by the optimal procedure.

It is interesting to investigate how the policy obtained by the heuristic procedure differs from the optimal policy for the cases with high percentage deviations $\Delta^{\mathrm{H-opt}}$. This is pictured in the bar plot in figure 3.18 where the problem instances with the highest percentage deviations of the average rewards were evaluated for problem classes 1 and 2. Figure 3.18 shows the FCFS policy and the policies obtained by the heuristic and the optimal procedures for each of the two problem instances.

The order classes n are sorted ascendingly by their relative profit margins m_n^{rel}. The bars of the FCFS policy show for each order class n the lowest capacity usage c where orders of this order class have to be rejected, i.e. the height of a bar of the FCFS policy corresponds to the heuristic threshold $\tau_n = l_n - u_n + 1$ where l_n and u_n are the lead time and the capacity usage of orders of class n, respectively.

It can be seen that in both problem instances, the heuristic procedure and the optimal procedure do not have any bars for the first few order classes with the lowest relative profit margins. This means that orders of these order classes are rejected in any case, independently of the current capacity utilization. Furthermore, figure 3.18 shows that the optimal policy generally accepts orders of more order classes than the heuristic policy, although these additional orders are only accepted when the current capacity utilization is relatively low.

Overall, one can conclude that the optimal policy seems to accept orders from more order classes than the heuristic policy, but that the heuristic policy accepts orders at higher capacity utilizations for the first order classes where orders are accepted. Thus, in order to improve the heuristic procedure, the search for better thresholds τ_n should move to accepting orders from more order classes, but at lower capacity utilizations.

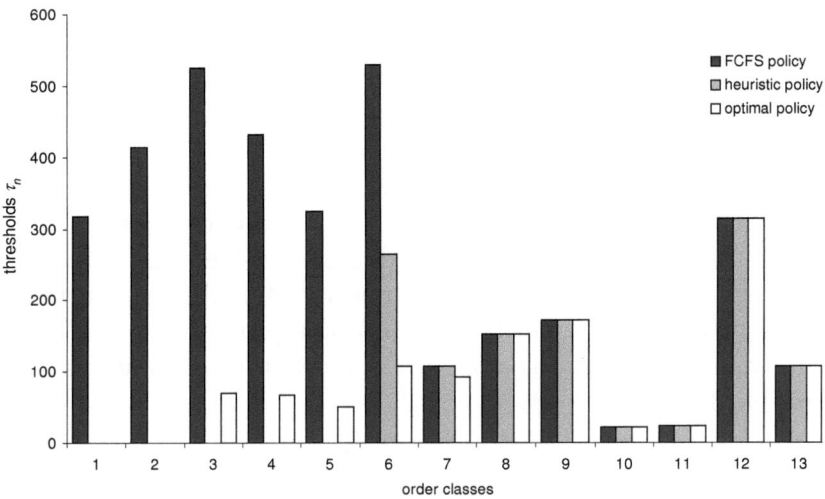

Problem Class 1: max$\{\Delta^{H-opt}\}$ = 4.2%

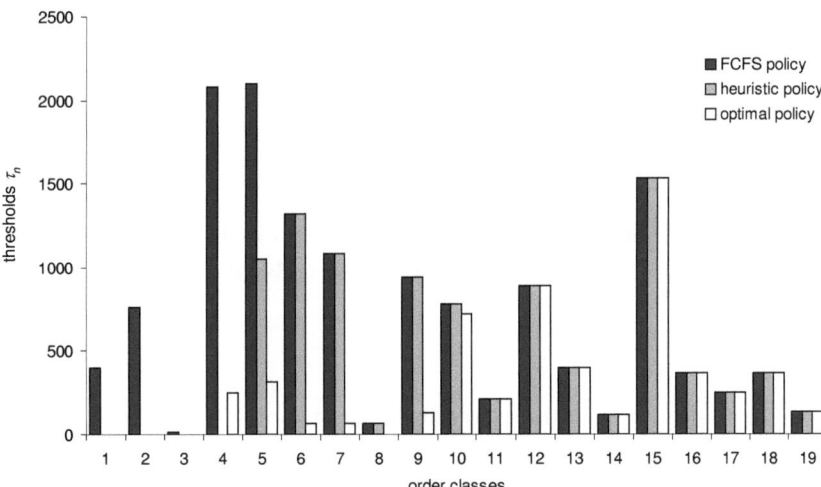

Problem Class 2: max$\{\Delta^{H-opt}\}$ = 5.0%

Figure 3.18: Two problem instances with the worst performance of the heuristic

3.5.2.1   Low Traffic Intensity

As the heuristic procedure starts out with a FCFS policy it is reasonable
to assume that the heuristic procedure will perform near-optimal when the
traffic intensity is low because the average rewards obtained by the optimal
policy do not differ much from the average rewards obtained by the FCFS
policy at low traffic intensities, see table 3.11. In order to verify this hypothesis, the heuristic procedure was applied to the problem instances that were
created in section 3.5.1.1 for a traffic intensity of 1. As the heuristic procedure has higher running times than the optimal procedure, only the first 500
scenarios were used for problem classes 1 and 2, though. The results can be
seen in table 3.16.

problem class →	1	2	3
problem instances	500	500	200
traffic intensity	1	1	1
average [%]	0.1	0.1	0.1
minimum [%]	0.0	0.0	0.0
maximum [%]	2.9	1.0	0.9
standard deviation [%]	0.2	0.1	0.2

Table 3.16: Percentage deviations $\Delta^{\text{H}-\text{opt}}$ of average rewards obtained by the
heuristic policy compared to average rewards obtained by the optimal policy
at $\rho = 1$

Table 3.16 shows that the percentage deviation of the average rewards is
around 0.1% on average. The distributions of the percentage deviations can
be seen in figure 3.19. The histograms show that most percentage deviations
are in the range between 0% and 0.1%. The maximum percentage deviation
of 2.9% for problem class 1 is higher than the maxima of problem classes 2
and 3. Thus it is interesting to analyze the heuristic policy for the problem
instance that results in this maximum percentage deviation.

Figure 3.20 shows the comparison of the optimal policy to the policy
obtained by the heuristic for this problem instance. In this problem instance,
the heuristic policy differs significantly from the optimal policy for the first
five order classes as it accepts more orders than the optimal policy. It is

remarkable that the optimal policy rejects orders from problem classes 4 and 5 completely. This might be due to the fact that the relative profit margins of the first five order classes are very similar as shown at the bottom of figure 3.20. Furthermore, the FCFS policy shows that problem classes 4 and 5 have a lower rejection limit $l_n - u_n + 1$ which might make it more advantageous to reject these order classes completely.

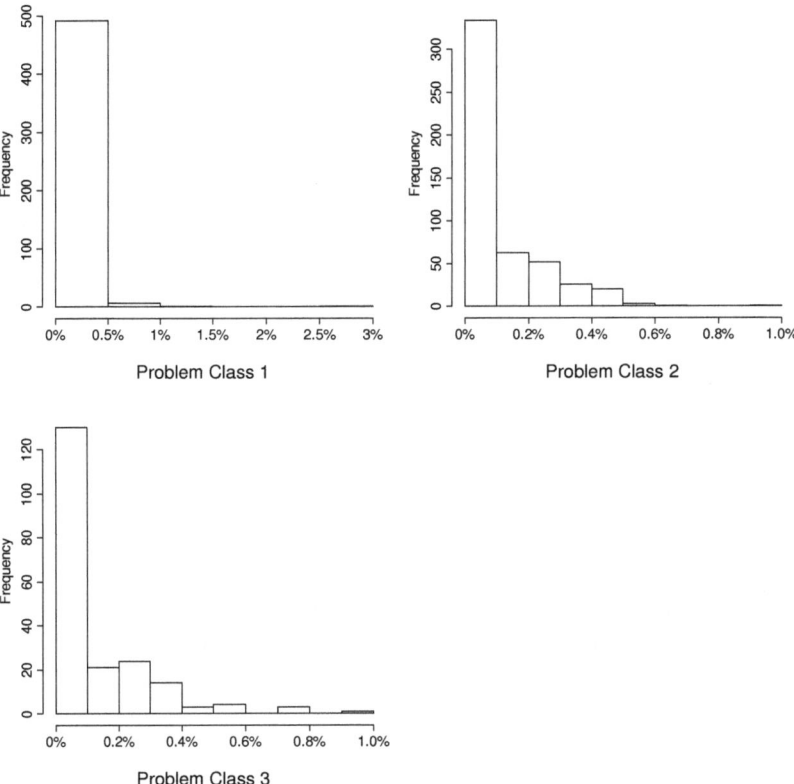

Figure 3.19: Histograms of the percentage deviations $\Delta^{\mathrm{H-opt}}$ of the optimal procedure compared to the heuristic procedure

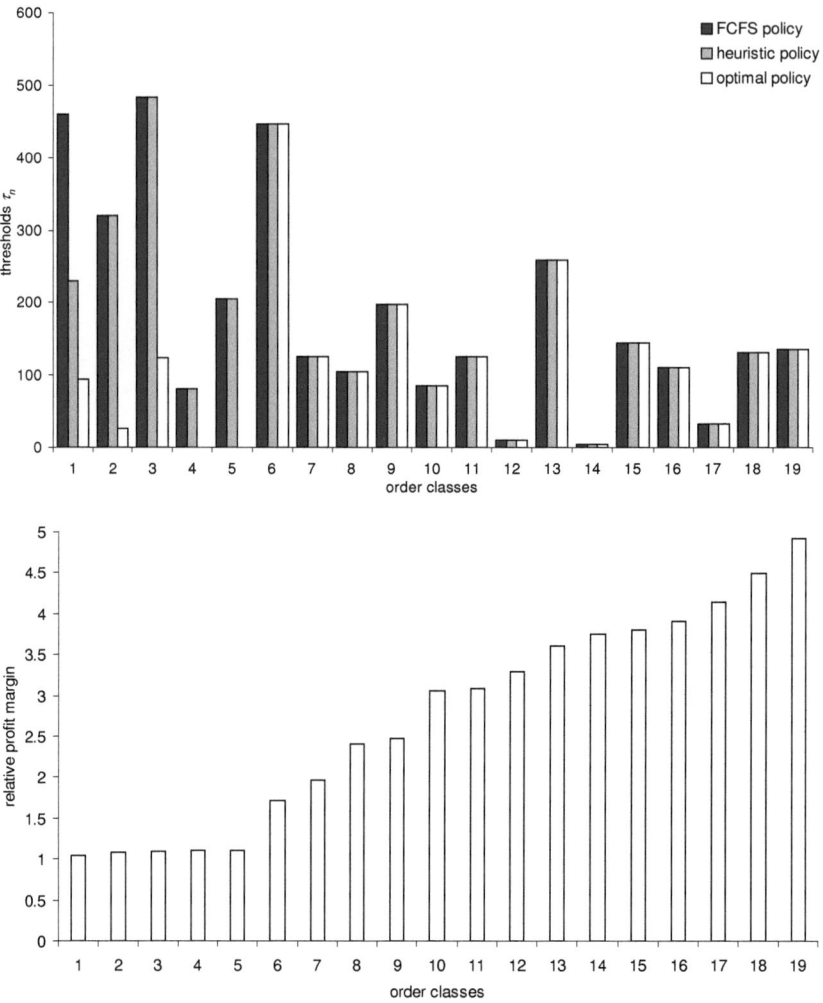

Figure 3.20: Comparing the FCFS policy, the heuristic policy and the optimal policy for the problem instance where $\Delta^{\mathrm{H-opt}} = 2.9\%$

3.5.2.2 High Traffic Intensity

The heuristic procedure was also tested at high traffic intensities. For this purpose, the scenarios were taken from section 3.5.1.1, this time with a traffic intensity of 2.5. The results can be seen in table 3.17.

problem class →	1	2	3
problem instances	500	500	200
traffic intensity	2.5	2.5	2.5
average [%]	0.4	0.5	0.6
minimum [%]	0.0	0.0	0.0
maximum [%]	6.3	8.1	7.9
standard deviation [%]	0.8	0.9	1.0

Table 3.17: Percentage deviations $\Delta^{\mathrm{H-opt}}$ at $\rho = 2.5$

Table 3.17 shows that the heuristic still performs satisfactorily at high traffic intensities although it turns out that $\Delta^{\mathrm{H-opt}}$ tends to be higher than in table 3.15. This is due to the fact that there is also a greater potential for revenue management at high traffic intensities, see section 3.5.1.1.

The histograms of $\Delta^{\mathrm{H-opt}}$ at high traffic intensities in figure 3.21 show that most percentage deviations lie in the $[0, 1]\%$ interval, demonstrating the usefulness of the heuristic procedure.

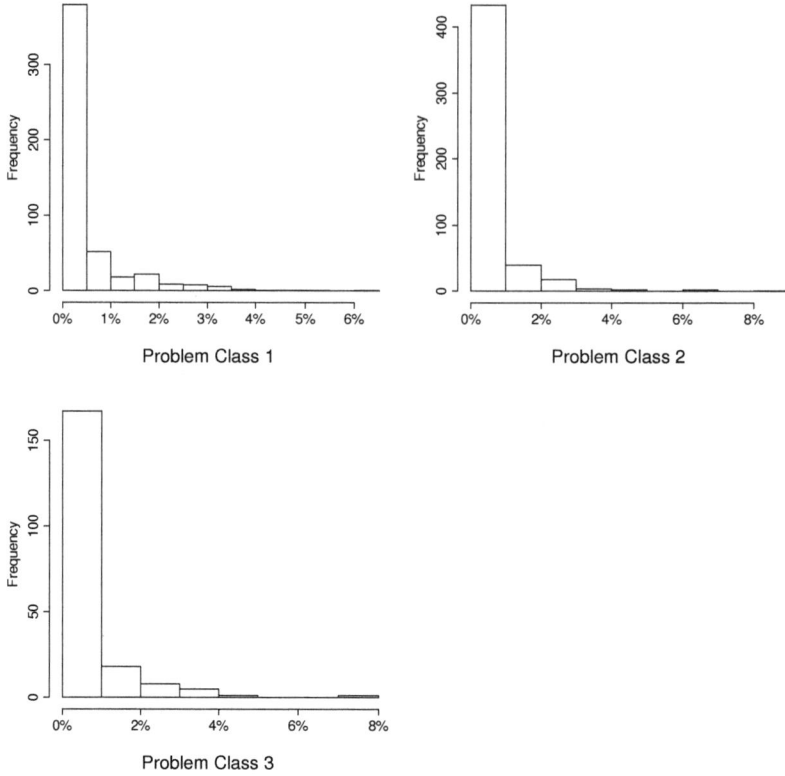

Figure 3.21: Histograms of $\Delta^{\mathrm{H-opt}}$ at high traffic intensities $\rho = 2.5$

3.5.3   Comparing the Heuristic to a FCFS Policy

For large problem instances, the optimal average reward could not be calculated within a reasonable time limit. Thus, the average reward of the
heuristic procedure was compared to the average reward of the FCFS policy
in order to demonstrate the usefulness of the heuristic procedure for large
problem instances.

Two more problem classes were used for comparing the heuristic procedure to the FCFS policy. They are shown in table 3.18.

problem class →	4	5
number of states	500,000	1,000,000
number of order classes	[10, 100]	[10, 100]
traffic intensity	[1, 2.5]	[1, 2.5]
maximum lead time	[4950, 45455]	[9901, 90909]

Table 3.18: Problem classes for comparing the heuristic procedure to a FCFS policy

Both average rewards were evaluated by simulation with a maximum relative error of $\gamma = 0.5\%$ and a confidence level of $1 - \alpha = 95\%$. The results of the comparison can be seen in table 3.19.

problem class →	4	5
problem instances	100	100
average [%]	1.2	1.4
minimum [%]	0.0	0.0
maximum [%]	16.8	16.0
standard deviation [%]	2.5	2.7
average running time FCFS [sec.]	253.5	537.8
average running time heuristic [sec.]	312.9	1615.7

Table 3.19: Percentage deviations $\Delta^{\text{FCFS-H}}$ of average rewards of the optimal policy compared to the FCFS policy

The percentage deviations $\Delta^{\text{FCFS-H}}$ were calculated by

$$\Delta^{\text{FCFS-H}} = \frac{g(\tilde{\pi}) - g(\pi^{\text{FCFS}})}{g(\pi^{\text{FCFS}})} \cdot 100\%$$

where $g(\tilde{\pi})$ and $g(\pi^{\text{FCFS}})$ were the average rewards obtained by simulation.

On average, the heuristic procedure fared better than the FCFS policy by 1.2% and 1.4%, but also greater improvements were recorded as can be seen by the maximum percentage deviations of about 16%.

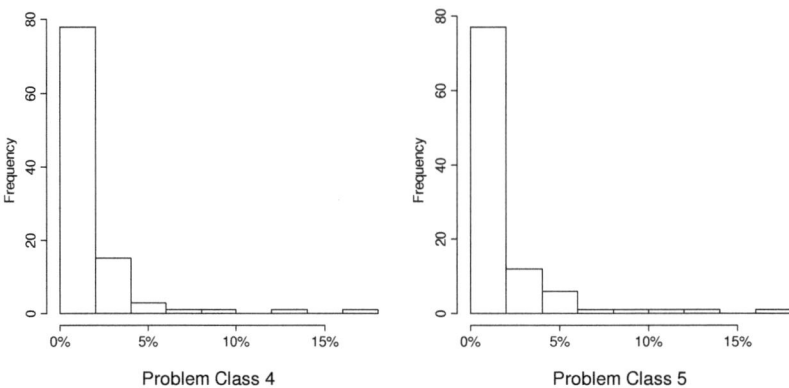

Figure 3.22: Histograms of the percentage deviations $\Delta^{\text{FCFS}-\text{H}}$ of the heuristic policy compared to the FCFS policy

The histograms in figure 3.22 give a more detailed view of the distributions of the percentage deviations.

Furthermore, the percentage distributions were studied under different traffic intensities. The results can be seen in table 3.20.

problem class $\rightarrow$		4	5
problem instances	$(\rho = 1/\rho = 2.5)$	100/100	100/100
average [%]	$(\rho = 1/\rho = 2.5)$	0.0/4.1	0.1/4.0
minimum [%]	$(\rho = 1/\rho = 2.5)$	0.0/0.0	0.0/0.0
maximum [%]	$(\rho = 1/\rho = 2.5)$	0.5/22.1	0.7/18.8
standard deviation [%]	$(\rho = 1/\rho = 2.5)$	0.1/4.2	0.1/4.1

Table 3.20: $\Delta^{\text{FCFS}-\text{H}}$ with different traffic intensities

As could be expected because of the results in sections 3.5.1.1 and 3.5.2.1, the percentage deviations were near zero for a traffic intensity of 1. For a traffic intensity of 2.5, table 3.20 shows that the heuristic procedure is able to produce significant improvements over a FCFS policy. This is further illustrated by the accompanying histograms in figure 3.23.

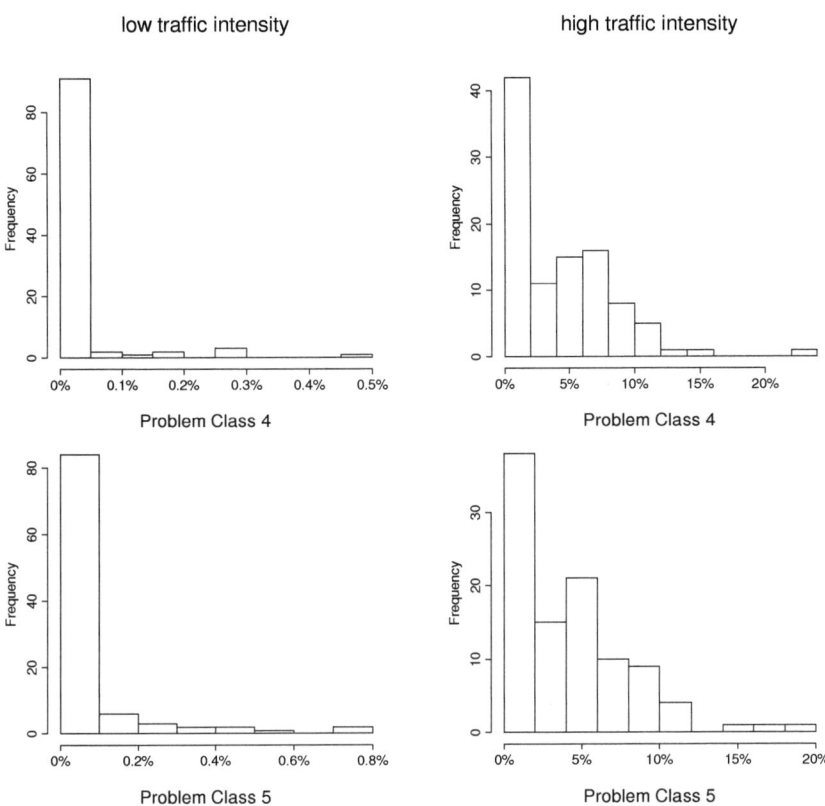

Figure 3.23: Histograms of the percentage deviations $\Delta^{\text{FCFS}-\text{H}}$ at varying traffic intensities

Overall, one can conclude for the numerical results that the heuristic procedure can produce significant improvements over a FCFS policy for large problem instances. The heuristic procedure also performs near-optimal for smaller problem instances, but the maximum percentage deviation $\Delta^{\text{H - opt}} = 8\%$ for high traffic intensities implies that the optimal procedure should be used for smaller problem instances. For large problem instances, the heuristic procedure is able to significantly improve the average reward of the FCFS policy at high traffic intensities and the heuristic procedure should thus be recommended to be used for an implementation with real-world problem instances.

Chapter 4

Limited Inventory Capacity

We now consider a manufacturing company with a single-level production capacity which manufactures only one product type and has a limited inventory capacity to store this product. Even if there is only one product type, the customers of this company have different preferences regarding the lead time that they are willing to accept for their orders. Some companies are in urgent need of the product while other companies can wait a little longer before receiving the product after placing their order. The orders that are placed at the company thus differ by their lead time, quantities and profit margins. The company now faces the decision which orders it should accept depending on the current inventory level and the current queue of accepted orders in front of its production capacity.

If the company accepts an order it has to decide by how many units of inventory it should fulfill the order and which portion of the order should be fulfilled by the production system. This decision problem is illustrated in figure 4.1.

© Springer Fachmedien Wiesbaden GmbH, part of Springer Nature 2009
F. Defregger, *Revenue Management for Manufacturing Companies*, Edition KWV,
https://doi.org/10.1007/978-3-658-24037-0_4

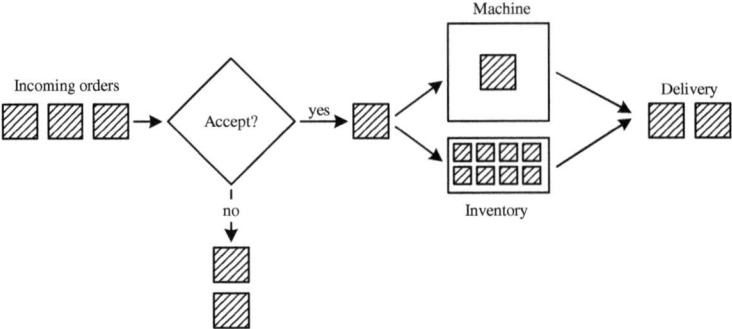

Figure 4.1: Decision problem with limited inventory capacity

Furthermore, the company has to decide how high it should set the maximum inventory level in the face of the current inventory holding cost. In the case of high inventory holding costs, it might be more profitable for the company not to use its full inventory capacity but rather fill up the inventory to a certain level or use no inventory at all. In the following we will present a model for this situation.

4.1   Model

4.1.1   Model Formulation

The decision problem that we consider is an order acceptance problem with limited inventory capacity that we model with an infinite-horizon discrete-time Markov decision process with the optimization criterion of maximizing the average reward per period. All orders that arrive at the manufacturing company can be associated with an order class $n \in \{1, \ldots, N\}$ where the number of order classes is given by N. In each period at most one order can arrive and the probability of an order of class n arriving in each period is given by $p_n, \sum_{n=1}^{N} p_n < 1$. Each order of class n has a profit margin m_n, a capacity usage of u_n discrete time periods, and a maximum lead time of l_n time periods. If an order is accepted, the complete fulfillment of that order will take place at the latest within l_n periods after accepting the order. Partial deliveries to the customers are taking place whenever possible and without any additional costs incurred. It is possible that no order arrives in a time period. This event is modeled by the dummy order class 0. The probability that no order arrives in a period is given by $p_0 = 1 - \sum_{n=1}^{N} p_n$, $p_0 > 0$. The system state of the production system is measured at the beginning of a discrete time period and is modeled by three state variables:

- $n \in \{0, \ldots, N\}$ is the class of the order that arrived in the beginning of the current time period

- c is the number of periods the machine is still busy because of orders that have been accepted in the past and have not been finished yet

- i is the current level of inventory. This state variable is measured in the number of periods that the machine needed to produce the inventory level i.

The state space of all possible system states (n, c, i) is denoted by S. The inventory has a maximum capacity of I^{max}. Furthermore, each unit that is on inventory for one period causes a holding cost of h monetary units.

The number of states $|S|$ is given by

$$|S| = (N + 1)(\max\{\max_n l_n, 1\})(I^{\text{max}} + 1) \tag{4.1}$$

In each state $(n, c, i) \in S$ the company can choose a decision from a set of decisions that depends on the state the system currently occupies. Basically, the company has four types of decisions at its disposal which are depicted in figure 4.2.

The four types of decisions are combinations of the decisions to accept or reject an incoming order and to raise the inventory level or not to raise it. If an order is accepted the company has to decide how many units of inventory should be used to fulfill this order. The possible decisions D for a given system state (n, c, i) are given as follows.

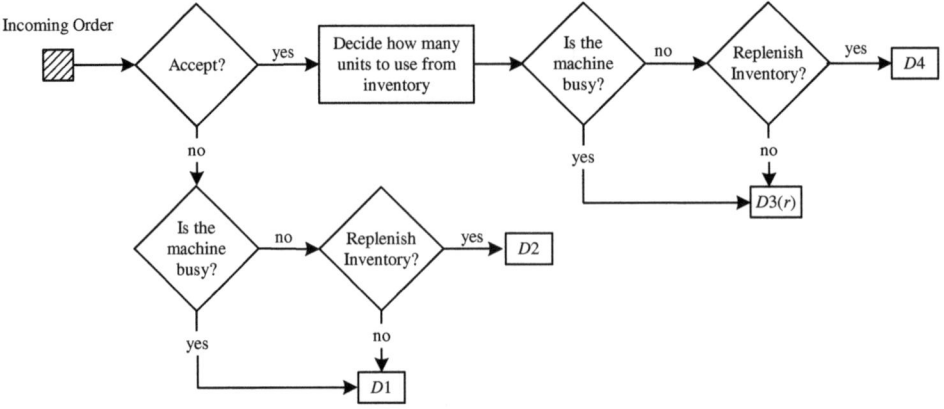

Figure 4.2: Sequence of decisions

$$D[(n, c, i)] = \begin{cases} D1 & := \text{"reject and do not raise inventory level"}, \forall(n, c, i) \in S \\ \\ D2 & := \text{"reject and raise inventory level"}, \\ & \forall(n, c, i) \in \{S : c = 0 \wedge i < I^{\max}\} \\ \\ D3(\iota) & := \text{"accept, do not raise inventory level and fulfill order by } \iota \\ & \text{units from the inventory"}, \forall \iota \in \\ & \{\iota_{\min}, \dots, \iota_{\max}\}, \forall(n, c, i) \in \{S : \\ & n > 0 \wedge (c + u_n \le l_n + i \vee u_n \le i)\} \\ \\ D4 & := \text{"accept, fill order by inventory only and raise inventory level"}, \\ & \forall(n, c, i) \in \{S : n > 0 \wedge c = 0 \wedge u_n \le i\} \end{cases}$$

The decisions can be further described as follows.

D1. The company always has the option of rejecting an incoming order and not to raise the inventory level.

D2. The company can always reject any incoming order but can use the production capacity during the current time period for raising the inventory level if there are currently no orders waiting for the machine and the current inventory level is below the maximum inventory level $I^{\max}$. As the company's decision only affects the current time period the inventory level i is raised by one unit.

D3(ι). This models the decision that the company accepts an order, takes ι units from the inventory to fulfill that order and does not raise the inventory level. The company can only accept an order if in fact an order has arrived ($n > 0$) and the current inventory and capacity booking levels i and c permit delivery of the order within its lead time l_n. Thus, it is feasible to accept an order if and only if $c + u_n \leq l_n + i \vee u_n \leq i$. Furthermore, it is feasible to use the machine to completely satisfy an order if and only if $c + u_n \leq l_n$. It is feasible to use the machine for partially satisfying an order if and only if $c < l_n$.

The number of units ι that are taken from the inventory to help fulfill the order is a decision variable and varies in the range between $\iota_{\min}$ and $\iota_{\max}$. The minimum amount of inventory that has to be used in order to fulfill the accepted order is given by $\iota_{\min} = \min\{\max\{0, c + u_n - l_n\}, u_n\}$ while the maximum amount that can be used to fulfill the order is given by $\iota_{\max} = \min\{i, u_n\}$. The range $[\iota_{\min}, \iota_{\max}]$ thus depends on the state (n, c, i) that the system occupies when the decision is taken.

One might argue that decision $D3(\iota)$ could be simplified and replaced by a decision $D3$ which just takes all the necessary inventory to fulfill an order and uses the machine if the inventory is not enough. Decision $D3(\iota)$ allows to reserve some inventory for highly profitable orders with very short lead times, though, which has a positive effect on the long-term average reward of the company.

D4. The company can accept order n, fulfill it by inventory only and at the same time raise the inventory level if and only if the production capacity is currently not occupied by any outstanding orders, i.e. $c = 0$, and the capacity requirement of the order u_n can be fulfilled by the current inventory level, i.e. $u_n \leq i$. As the company's decision only affects the current time period the inventory level i is raised by one unit.

The reward R in a given system state $(n, c, i) \in S$ that the company receives in a discrete time period results from the decision the company took in that period:

$$
\begin{aligned}
R^{D1} &= -h\,i \\
R^{D2} &= -h\,i \\
R^{D3(\iota)} &= m_n - h(i - \iota) \\
R^{D4} &= m_n - h(i - u_n)
\end{aligned}
$$

It is assumed that if a decision to raise the inventory level has been taken, i.e. decision $D2$ or $D4$, the inventory level will have increased by the end of the period. Thus the additional inventory holding costs which result from the increase of the inventory level will only apply in the next period. If the company partially or completely fulfills an order by inventory, i.e. decision $D3(\iota)$ or $D4$, the inventory holding costs decrease accordingly.

The transition probabilities P show which states can be reached from a state (n, c, i) once a certain decision has been taken.

$$
P^{D1}[(n, c, i), (m, \max\{c - 1, 0\}, i)] = p_m, \forall (n, c, i) \in S, \forall m \in \{0, \ldots, N\}
$$

If the company rejects an order and does not raise the inventory level (decision $D1$), the capacity booking level c is reduced by one in the next period. If c has reached zero, it stays zero if the company continues to reject orders. If the company decides for $D2$ the inventory level increases by one unit:

$$
P^{D2}[(n, 0, i), (m, 0, i + 1)] =
\begin{cases}
p_m, & \forall n \in \{0, \ldots, N\}, \\
 & \forall m \in \{0, \ldots, N\}, \\
 & \forall i \in \{0, \ldots, I^{\max} - 1\} \\
0, & \text{else}
\end{cases}
$$

If the company accepts an order and uses ι units from the inventory to fulfill it, the capacity booking level c and the inventory level i are updated accordingly:

$$
P^{D3(\iota)}[(n, c, i), (m, \max\{0, c + u_n - 1 - \iota\}, i - \iota)] =
$$

$$
=
\begin{cases}
p_m, & \forall \iota \in \{\iota_{\min}, \ldots, \iota_{\max}\}, \\
 & \forall (n, c, i) \in \{S : n > 0 \wedge c + u_n \le l_n + i \vee u_n \le i\}, \\
 & \forall m \in \{0, \ldots, N\} \\
0, & \text{else}
\end{cases}
$$

If the company accepts an order, uses only the inventory to fulfill it and raises the inventory level, the system state evolves as follows:

$$
P^{D4}[(n,0,i),(m,0,i-u_n+1)] = \begin{cases} p_m, & \forall n \in \{\{1,\ldots,N\} : u_n \leq i\}, \\ & \forall m \in \{0,\ldots,N\}, \\ & \forall i \in \{0,\ldots,I^{\max}-1\} \\ 0, & \text{else} \end{cases}
$$

All system states, decisions, transition probabilities and rewards specify an infinite-horizon, discrete-time Markov decision process. In order to determine which solution procedure can be applied, this Markov decision process has to be classified.

4.1.2 Model Classification

As we will describe below, the Markov decision process can be classified as multichain and communicating. A deterministic policy specifies which decision is taken at each state every time the system occupies this state. Once a policy has been selected, the Markov decision process becomes a discrete-time Markov reward process with a corresponding transition probability matrix.

Following Puterman (1994), the Markov decision process that we specified in the previous section can be classified as multichain as there exists at least one policy which induces two or more closed irreducible classes. This can be seen in figure 4.3 which shows the stochastic process resulting from such a policy. The policy-maker can choose an arbitrary inventory threshold $\tilde{\imath} \in \{1,\ldots,I^{\max}\}$. If the system's inventory level is below $\tilde{\imath}$, the policy prescribes that the inventory level is never raised above $\tilde{\imath}$. If the inventory level is above $\tilde{\imath}$, the inventory level is never decreased below $\tilde{\imath}$. Thus this policy induces a multichain transition matrix and the Markov decision process can be classified as multichain.

The Markov decision process can also be classified as communicating. A Markov decision process is called communicating if there exists a single policy under which a is accessible from b for every pair of states $a, b \in S$. To show that this Markov decision process is communicating consider the policy π^{com} that always raises the inventory level whenever possible and accepts all incoming orders. Furthermore, the policy satisfies the orders of order class $m = \arg\max_n l_n$ only by the machine and not by the inventory, and all

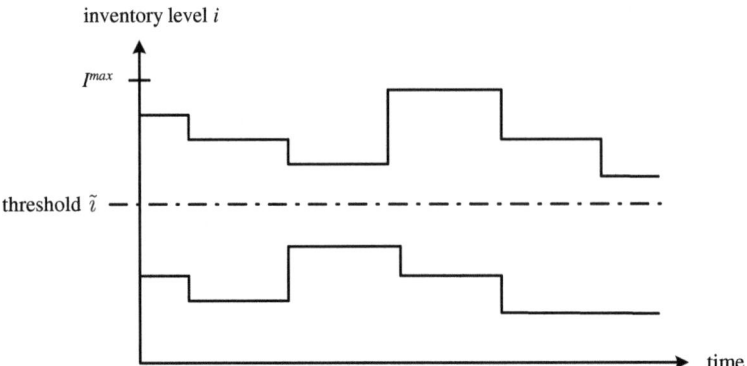

Figure 4.3: Stochastic process resulting from a policy which induces a multichain structure

other orders of classes $n \neq m$ are satisfied by the inventory if available and otherwise by the resource.

We will first show that the state variables n, c and i can realize all possible values independently of each other.

- **Order class n.** With regards to the state variable n, the Markov decision process is communicating because any order of class $n \in \{0, \ldots, N\}$ can arrive in all time periods.

- **Capacity booking level c.** Under any policy the capacity booking level c can always decrease to 0 if for a very long number of periods no orders arrive which is possible because of the condition $p_0 > 0$. On the other hand, there is a positive probability that the booking level c can reach its maximum $c^{\max} = (\max_n l_n) - 1$ if an order of class m arrives in every period. Thus, all possible capacity booking levels $c \in \{0, \ldots, c^{\max}\}$ can be reached.

- **Inventory level i.** By a similar argument, the state variable i can also realize all possible values. By fulfilling all incoming orders of classes $n \neq m$ by the inventory as far as possible, the inventory level i can be brought to zero. On the other hand, if no orders arrive for a very long period the capacity booking level c will decrease to zero and the inventory level can be raised to its maximum level $I^{\max}$.

We still have to show that all states and thus all possible combinations of n, c and i can be reached under policy π^{com}. First we will show that all combinations of the minimum and maximum values of the state variable c and i can be reached from any state (n, c, i) under policy π^{com}.

It is obvious that the state $(0, 0, I^{\max})$ can be reached from any state (n, c, i) if no orders arrive for a very long time. Once state $(0, 0, I^{\max})$ has been reached, an order of any class n can arrive and thus all states $(n, 0, I^{\max})$ can be reached.

Furthermore, the states $(n, c^{\max}, 0)$ can be reached from any state if orders of class $n \neq m$ arrive in every period to decrease the inventory level to zero and then orders of any class arrive in every period to increase c. Once $c^{\max}$ has been reached, any order of class n can arrive and thus any state $(n, c^{\max}, 0)$ can be reached.

Now consider the states $(n, c^{\max}, I^{\max})$. These states can be reached under policy π^{com} from any state by considering a long period of time where no order arrives and the inventory level rises to $I^{\max}$. Then, if only orders of class m arrive for a long time, the inventory level will not change while c will rise to its maximum $c^{\max}$. Once the state $(m, c^{\max}, I^{\max})$ has been reached, any order of class n can arrive and thus any state $(n, c^{\max}, I^{\max})$ can be reached under policy π^{com}.

Then consider the states $(n, 0, 0)$. These states might be difficult to reach under policy π^{com} because the inventory level i is raised whenever $c = 0$. But consider the case that the stochastic process has reached the state $(n, c^{\max}, 0)$, see two paragraphes above. Now consider the stochastic path that results from no orders arriving at all for a long period of time. Then, c will decrease to zero as well and the state $(0, 0, 0)$ will be reached. From this state, any state $(n, 0, 0)$ can be reached.

We now have shown that all combinations of extreme values of the state variables c, i.e. 0 and $c^{\max}$, and i, i.e. 0 and $I^{\max}$, can be reached under policy π^{com} from any state (n, c, i). It remains to show that all combinations of values between the extreme values of c and i can be reached under policy π^{com} as well.

Any value of $i \in \{1, \ldots, I^{\max} - 1\}$ can be reached if the stochastic process is in the state $(0, 0, 0)$ and no orders arrive while the inventory level rises under policy π^{com}. Once any value of i has been reached and the stochastic process reaches the state $(0, 0, i)$, any value of c can be reached if only orders of class m begin to arrive. As c will rise by $u_m - 1$ each time an order of class m has arrived, the values of c between the multiples of $u_m - 1$ can be reached if no orders arrive in between. Thus, all possible values of c can be reached from any inventory level i under policy π^{com}.

As we have shown that all possible outcomes of the state variables n, c and i can be realized under policy π^{com} the Markov decision process can be classified as communicating.

As the Markov decision process is multichain and communicating, the unichain versions of solution procedures like value iteration, policy iteration or linear programming do not apply. Instead, the communicating versions of these solution procedures have to be used. For the inventory model, the communicating value iteration method was selected because of its relative simplicity with regards to implementation compared to the other solution procedures. But in order to be able to use value iteration, one has to show that the transition matrices of optimal policies are aperiodical, see Puterman (1994).

We now show that all possible policies induce aperiodical transition matrices. First consider the unichain case, i.e. the decision maker does not set a threshold $\tilde{\imath}$ as seen in figure 4.3 and it is possible that the inventory level can always decrease to zero. A transition matrix is aperiodical if one system state in each recurrent class of the transition matrix can be found which allows a transition into itself. To find these states one can make the assumption that no orders arrive during a large number of time periods which is possible because of the condition $p_0 > 0$. Then the capacity booking level c will decrease to 0 and the stochastic process will remain in the states $(n, 0, i)$. Now, two cases depending on the inventory policy can be distinguished. If the policy does not prescribe to fill up the inventory level for any $i \in \{0, \ldots, I^{\mathrm{max}} - 1\}$ in the system state $(n, 0, i)$, the system state will not change and the transition matrix will thus be aperiodic. If the policy prescribes to fill up the inventory level until I^{max}, the inventory level will increase to I^{max}. If no order arrives ($n = 0$) which is possible because of the assumption $p_0 > 0$, the state will make a transition into itself as the state variables n, c and i remain unchanged. Thus the transition matrix is aperiodic.

This argument can be extended to multichain policies as well, see figure 4.4. No matter in which closed recurrent class the stochastic process is evolving, the inventory level can always rise to its maximum with respect to the recurrent class and then there is a positive probability that the system state remains unchanged. Thus, for multichain policies all possible transition matrices are aperiodic as well.

As we have shown all possible policies to be aperiodic, we can use the communicating value iteration algorithm to find the optimal policy for the Markov decision process. As we will show in the numerical results, the value iteration algorithm does not converge in a reasonable amount of time for large problem instances, though. Thus, the need for a heuristic procedure arises for large problem instances.

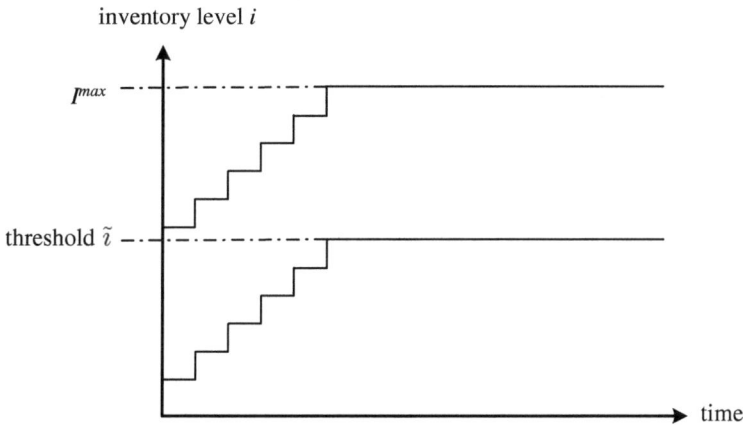

Figure 4.4: Example for a multichain policy which induces two aperiodic recurrent classes

4.2 A Heuristic Procedure

The heuristic procedure consists of two parts. In the first part, a heuristic inventory policy is determined while in the second part, a heuristic capacity allocation policy is identified. The first part extends the heuristic procedure described in Defregger and Kuhn (2007).

4.2.1   Determining a Maximum Inventory Level

It might not be advantageous for a company to always replenish its inventory to its full inventory capacity $I^{\max}$ because of high inventory holding costs or low demand for its products. Thus, a maximum inventory level $\tilde{I}$ has to be determined that ensures that the inventory level will not rise above $\tilde{I}$ and will improve the average reward in order to reflect the inventory holding costs and demand patterns. The company will then only replenish its inventory to $\tilde{I} \in \{0, \ldots, I^{\max}\}$ instead of always replenishing its inventory to $I^{\max}$. In order to determine such an inventory level $\tilde{I}$, the heuristic procedure compares different maximum inventory levels for a FCFS policy that accepts all orders if possible and chooses the inventory level $\tilde{I}$ that generated the highest average reward for this FCFS policy.

The heuristic procedure assumes that the average reward is a concave function of the maximum inventory level $\tilde{I}$. This is illustrated in figure 4.5 which shows that at high inventory holding costs, the average reward $g(\tilde{I})$ can even become negative for a high maximum inventory level as the inventory holding costs outweigh the revenues which are received by fulfilling incoming orders.

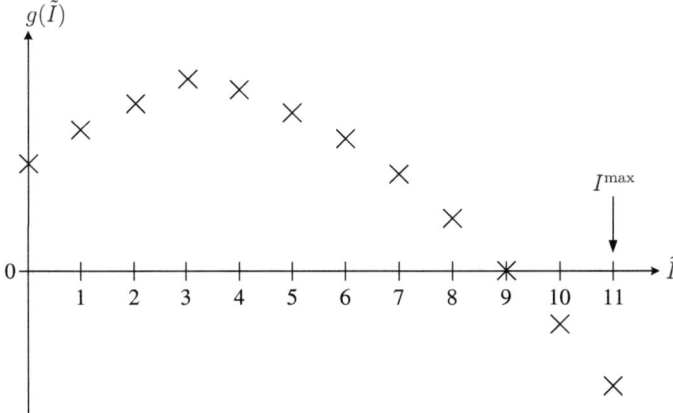

Figure 4.5: Assumption of the average reward $g(\tilde{I})$ depending on the maximum inventory level $\tilde{I}$

The procedure to determine $\tilde{I}$ is outlined in algorithm 4.1.

Algorithm 4.1 Determine a maximum inventory level

$\underline{I} \leftarrow 0, \overline{I} \leftarrow I^{\max}, I_1 \leftarrow 0, I_2 \leftarrow I^{\max}, \tilde{I} \leftarrow 0$

compare I_1 and I_2 by simulation and estimate $\hat{g}(I_1)$ and $\hat{g}(I_2)$

$\hat{g}(\underline{I}) \leftarrow \hat{g}(I_1), \hat{g}(\overline{I}) \leftarrow \hat{g}(I_2)$

repeat

    if $\hat{g}(I_1) \geq \hat{g}(I_2)$ **then**

        $\overline{I} \leftarrow I_2, \tilde{I} \leftarrow I_1$

    else if $\hat{g}(I_2) > \hat{g}(I_1)$ **then**

        $\underline{I} \leftarrow I_1, \tilde{I} \leftarrow I_2$

    end if

    if $|(\overline{I} - \tilde{I}) - (\tilde{I} - \underline{I})| \leq 1$ **then** $\{\overline{I}$ and $\underline{I}$ have equal distance to $\tilde{I}\}$

        if $\hat{g}(\overline{I}) > \hat{g}(\underline{I})$ **then**

            $I_1 \leftarrow \tilde{I}, I_2 \leftarrow \tilde{I} + \lfloor (\overline{I} - \tilde{I})/2 \rfloor$

        else

            $I_2 \leftarrow \tilde{I}, I_1 \leftarrow \tilde{I} - \lfloor (\tilde{I} - \underline{I})/2 \rfloor$

        end if

    else $\{\overline{I}$ and $\underline{I}$ do not have equal distance to $\tilde{I}\}$

        if $\tilde{I} - \underline{I} < \overline{I} - \tilde{I}$ **then** $\{\tilde{I}$ is closer to $\underline{I}$ than to $\overline{I}\}$

            $I_1 \leftarrow \tilde{I}, I_2 \leftarrow \tilde{I} + \lfloor (\overline{I} - \tilde{I})/2 \rfloor$

        else if $\overline{I} - \tilde{I} < \tilde{I} - \underline{I}$ **then** $\{\tilde{I}$ is closer to $\overline{I}$ than to $\underline{I}\}$

            $I_2 \leftarrow \tilde{I}, I_1 \leftarrow \tilde{I} - \lfloor (\tilde{I} - \underline{I})/2 \rfloor$

        end if

    end if

    compare I_1 and I_2 by simulation and estimate $\hat{g}(I_1)$ and $\hat{g}(I_2)$

until $I_2 - I_1 \leq 1$

if $\hat{g}(I_1) \geq \hat{g}(I_2)$ **then**

    $\tilde{I} \leftarrow I_1$

else

    $\tilde{I} \leftarrow I_2$

end if

It starts by initializing $\tilde{I}$, the maximum inventory level that generates the highest average reward so far, a lower bound $\underline{I}$ and an upper bound $\overline{I}$ for $\tilde{I}$, and the two maximum inventory levels I_1 and I_2 that are compared first. The heuristic procedure then compares the average rewards that result from FCFS policies with a maximum inventory level of zero and a maximum inventory level with the inventory capacity $I^{\max}$. This is illustrated in figure 4.6.

After that, a procedure is repeated which consists of the following steps. First, the lower and the upper bound and $\tilde{I}$, the best maximum inventory level found so far, are updated. In a second step, the maximum inventory levels I_1 and I_2 that should be compared next are determined. To set I_1 and I_2, it is checked wether the updated bounds have roughly the same distance to $\tilde{I}$. If this is the case I_1 and I_2 are set depending on the current values of the average rewards $\hat{g}(\underline{I})$ and $\hat{g}(\overline{I})$ of the bounds $\underline{I}$ and $\overline{I}$. An example is given in figure 4.7.

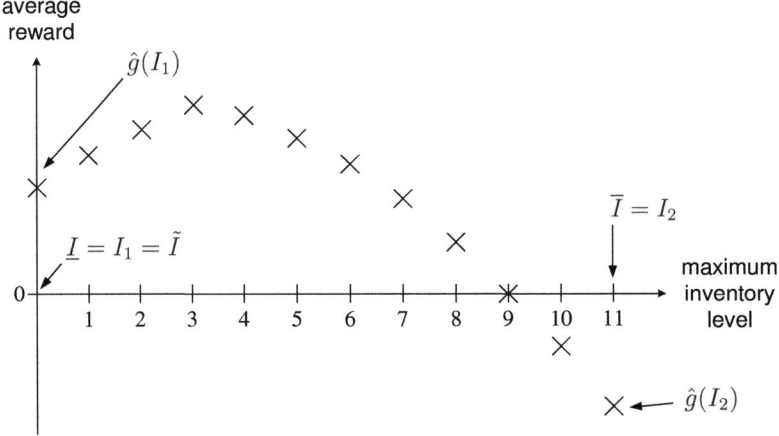

Figure 4.6: Initializing the heuristic procedure

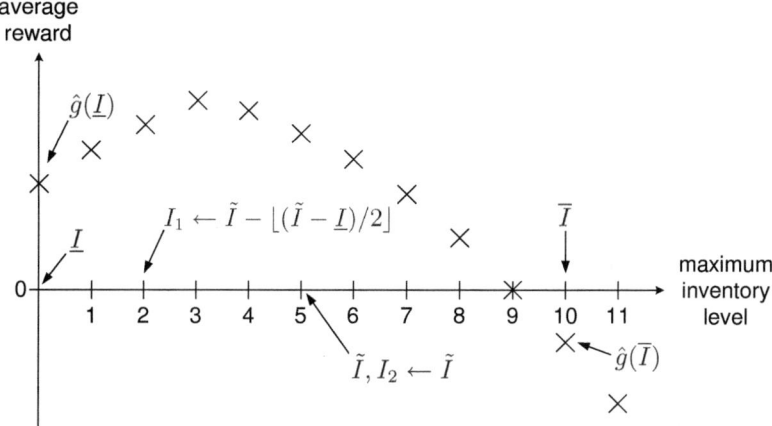

Figure 4.7: Setting I_1 and I_2 if $\tilde{I}$ has the same distance to $\underline{I}$ and $\overline{I}$

If the bounds $\underline{I}$ and $\overline{I}$ do not have the same distance to $\tilde{I}$, I_1 and I_2 are set depending on the distances of the bounds to $\tilde{I}$ which is illustrated in figure 4.8.

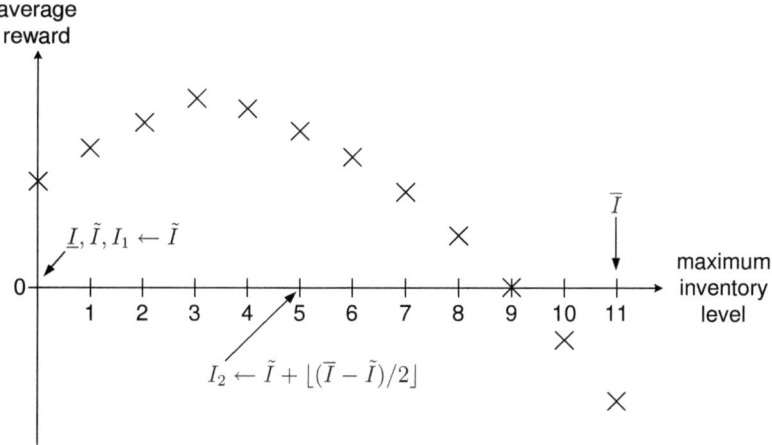

Figure 4.8: Setting I_1 and I_2 if $\tilde{I}$ does not have the same distance to $\underline{I}$ and $\overline{I}$

The procedure continues until the difference between I_1 and I_2 becomes smaller or equal than 1. The procedure results in the maximum inventory level $\tilde{I}$ until which the company will replenish its inventory. Thus, the stochastic reward process resulting from any simulated policy can not visit any states with an inventory level greater than $\tilde{I}$ any more as the warmup phase of each simulation replication starts with the state $(0,0,0)$, i.e. with no order arrived and a capacity and inventory level of zero.

Two FCFS policies with different maximum inventory levels I_1 and I_2 are compared by simulation and the paired-t confidence interval approach which was outlined in section 3.4.

4.2.2   Finding a Capacity Allocation Policy

After the maximum inventory $\tilde{I}$ has been determined, the heuristic procedure tries to find a good policy regarding the acceptance and rejection of incoming orders. This is done similarly to the heuristic procedure presented for the basic model in the previous chapter. The order classes are sorted ascendingly by their relative profit margins m_n/u_n and the heuristic starts to reject orders from the order classes with the lowest relative profit margins.

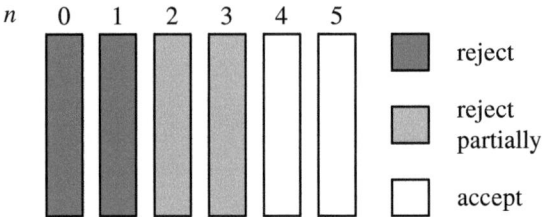

Figure 4.9: Accepting and rejecting order classes

A difference to the basic model is the definition of "partially rejecting" an order class. Figure 4.10 illustrates the concept of partial rejection of a certain order class, e.g. order class 2 or 3 in figure 4.9. We consider a hypothetical order class n that is partially rejected and has a capacity usage u_n of 3 units and a lead time l_n of 4 time periods. The maximum inventory level $\tilde{I}$ is 7. It can be seen in figure 4.10 that there are some states in which the company is forced to reject orders and cannot decide otherwise because it cannot deliver the product within the lead time l_n wanted by the customer, even if there is some inventory i on hand.

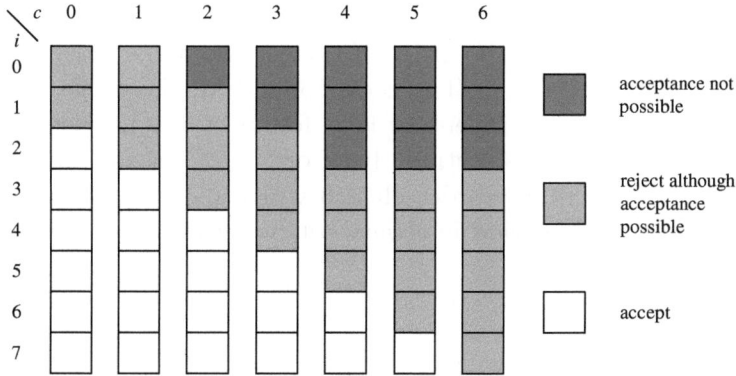

Figure 4.10: Partial rejection of order class n, $l_n = 4$, $u_n = 3$

The dummy order class 0, which represents the case that no order arrives in a given period is always set to rejection. The exemplary policy in figure 4.9 rejects order class 1, the order class with the lowest relative profit margin, in all system states even if it could be accepted in some system states. This rejection of order class 1 might increase the average reward of the company in order to reserve capacity for order classes with higher profit margins. Order classes 2 and 3 are only partially rejected which means that they are accepted in some system states but rejected in all other system states, even if they could be accepted in some of those other system states. Order classes 4 and 5 which have the highest relative profit margins are accepted in all system states where acceptance is possible. The optimal policy will be the optimal combination of which order classes are completely rejected, which order classes are partially rejected and which order classes are fully accepted.

In order to develop a heuristic procedure it is helpful to approximate each policy of mapping an action to each state by an N-dimensional vector $\theta^T = (\tau_0, \tau_1, \ldots, \tau_N)$. The element τ_n specifies what the minimum inventory level i is for accepting an order when $c = 0$, e.g. in figure 4.10, $\tau_n = 2$. For $c > 0$ the decision at what minimum inventory level to accept or reject an order is given by $\tau_n + c$, e.g. with $\tau_n = 2$ and $c = 1$, the order is accepted at a minimum inventory level i of 3 units, see figure 4.10.

Each τ_n thus specifies exactly in which states orders of class n should be accepted and in which states they should be rejected. The lower bound of the range for each element τ_n is $\max\{0, u_n - l_n\}$ as this is the minimum inventory needed to accept the order of class n when the machine capacity is not booked out, i. e., $c = 0$. The upper bound for the range of each τ_n is $\tilde{I}$, where $\tilde{I}$ is the maximum inventory level found by the heuristic procedure as described in the previous section. If all orders of class n are rejected, τ_n is set to $\tilde{I} + 1$. The dummy order class 0 which models the event that no order arrives in a given period is always set to rejection, so $\tau_0 \leftarrow \tilde{I} + 1$ for any heuristic policy.

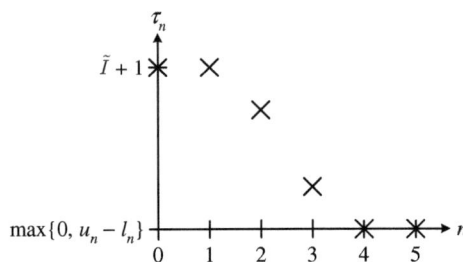

Figure 4.11: Policy approximation

Figure 4.11 shows how a policy with five order classes is approximated by the vector $\theta^T = (\tau_0, \tau_1, \ldots, \tau_5)$. In this example, the order class with the lowest relative profit margin m_n/u_n is completely rejected while order classes 2 and 3 are partially rejected. Order classes 4 and 5 are fully accepted.

Denote by π the policy that the order classes $n \in \{0, \ldots, \pi\}$ are completely rejected and the order classes $n \in \{\pi + 1, \ldots, N\}$ are completely accepted. The idea of the heuristic is to evaluate various policies and find good policies by simulation comparisons. Each policy π results in a Markov reward process with an associated average reward per period $g(\pi)$ whose estimate $\hat{g}(\pi)$ can be obtained by simulation. The heuristic starts by comparing policies $\pi = 0$ and $\pi = 1$ by simulation (see figure 4.12). If $\hat{g}(0) > \hat{g}(1)$ policy 0 of accepting all order classes is accepted as the optimal policy and the heuristic stops. Otherwise, $\pi \to \pi + 1$ and the procedure continues likewise until $\hat{g}(\pi) > \hat{g}(\pi + 1)$. At that point, policy π has the highest average reward of all policies compared so far, see figure 4.13 for an example.

Now, the heuristic tries to further optimize policy π by comparing it to

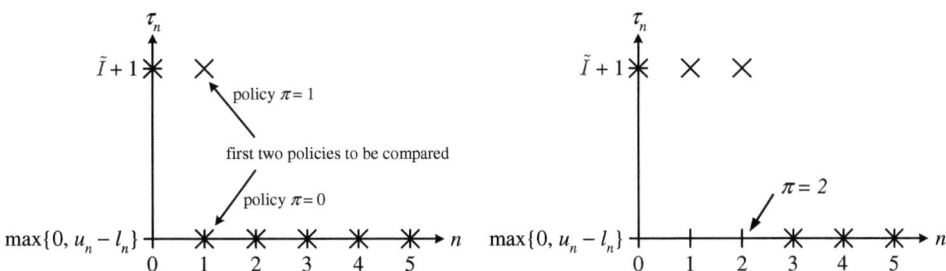

Figure 4.12: Comparing policies   Figure 4.13: Policy $\pi = 2$

policy π^+ which is obtained by setting

$$\tau_{\pi+1} \leftarrow \lfloor \frac{\tilde{I} + 1 - \max\{0, u_{\pi+1} - l_{\pi+1}\}}{2} \rfloor + \max\{0, u_{\pi+1} - l_{\pi+1}\},$$

see figure 4.14. If $\widehat{g}(\pi^+) > \widehat{g}(\pi)$ policy π^+ is accepted to be $\tilde{\pi}$, the best policy found by the heuristic. Otherwise, policy π is compared to policy π^- which is obtained by setting

$$\tau_{\pi} \leftarrow \lfloor \frac{\tilde{I} + 1 - \max\{0, u_{\pi} - l_{\pi}\}}{2} \rfloor + \max\{0, u_{\pi} - l_{\pi}\}.$$

If $\widehat{g}(\pi^-) > \widehat{g}(\pi)$ policy π^- is set to be $\tilde{\pi}$, otherwise policy π is set to be $\tilde{\pi}$.

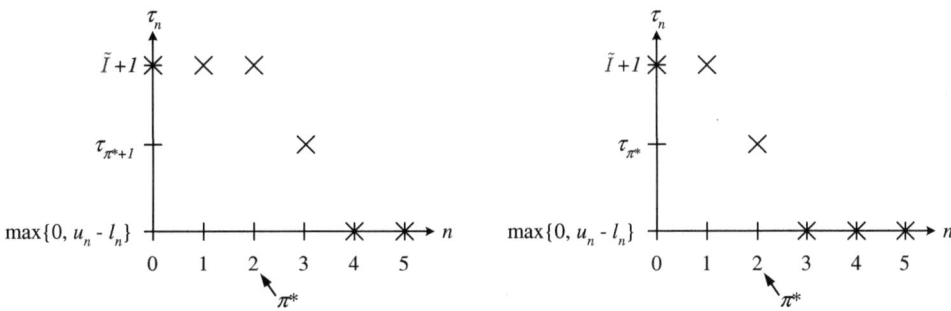

Figure 4.14: Policies π^+ and π^-

Two policies are again compared by using the paired-t confidence interval approach, see section 3.4.

4.3   Numerical Results

4.3.1   Creating Problem Instances

The problem instances that are generated for the model with a maximum inventory capacity are created in a similar way as for the basic model as described in section 3.1.4. The only difference lies with additional input parameters for the procedure to randomly create a problem instance. These additional input parameters are the inventory capacity I^{max} and a lower bound $\underline{h}$ and an upper bound $\overline{h}$ for the holding cost h. First, the inventory holding cost h is drawn from a $[\underline{h}, \overline{h}]$ uniform distribution. After that, the traffic intensity is drawn from a $[1, 2.5]$ uniform distribution. Then, the maximum lead time l^{max} is calculated by

$$l^{\text{max}} = \lfloor |S|/((N+1)\, I^{\text{max}}) \rfloor$$

where $|S|$ is the desired number of states, N is the number of order classes and I^{max} is the maximum inventory capacity of the problem instance. The real number of states that the problem instance will have is calculated by

$$|S|^{\text{real}} = (N+1)(\max\{l^{\text{max}}, 1\})(I^{\text{max}} + 1)$$

and will often differ a bit from the desired number of states because the number of states, the maximum lead time, the number of order classes and the maximum inventory capacity all have to be integer numbers.

After $|S|^{\text{real}}$ has been determined, the procedure follows the procedure to create a problem instance for the basic model which is described in section 3.1.4. The only difference to the procedure for the basic model is that the lead time of an order class can now be drawn to be less than the order class usage. The lower bound $\underline{l_n}$ of the lead time of each order class is given by $\underline{l_n} = \max\{u_n - I^{\text{max}}, 0\}$ and each lead time is drawn from a uniform $[\underline{l_n},\ l^{\text{max}}]$ distribution.

4.3.2   Comparing the Optimal Policy to a FCFS Policy

The average reward of the ϵ-optimal policy obtained by value iteration was compared to the average reward of a FCFS policy in order to evaluate the potential benefits of using revenue management. Under the FCFS policy all orders are accepted whenever possible. In order to prevent negative average rewards of the FCFS policy due to high inventory holding costs, a simple heuristic was implemented before the average reward of the FCFS policy was evaluated.

This simple heuristic compared the average reward of using a maximum inventory level of $I^{\max}$ versus using a maximum inventory level of zero. In the case of high inventory costs the FCFS policy will operate with a maximum inventory level of zero and in the case of low inventory costs the FCFS policy will operate with a maximum inventory level of $I^{\max}$. After a maximum inventory level $\tilde{I}$ had been chosen, the average reward of the FCFS policy was evaluated by simulation with a confidence level of 95% and a maximum relative error of 5%. Calculations were done on a 733 MHz Intel Pentium machine with 392 MB of memory. The optimal policy was determined by value iteration where ϵ was set to 0.5%.

The problem classes that were used for comparing the FCFS policy to the ϵ-optimal policy are displayed in table 4.1.

problem class $\rightarrow$	1	2	3
number of states	10,000	50,000	100,000
number of order classes	[5, 10]	[5, 20]	[5, 30]
maximum inventory capacity	20	30	50
inventory holding cost	[0.01, 1]	[0.01, 1]	[0.01, 1]
relative profit margin	[1, 5]	[1, 5]	[1, 5]
traffic intensity	[1, 2.5]	[1, 2.5]	[1, 2.5]
maximum lead time	[43, 79]	[77, 269]	[63, 327]

Table 4.1: Problem classes for comparing the ϵ-optimal policy to a FCFS policy

Three problem classes with 10,000, 50,000 and 100,000 states were chosen. The number of order classes for each problem instance was drawn from a uniform distribution which depended on the problem class. The maximum inventory level was fixed for each problem class. The inventory holding cost was drawn from a [0.01, 1] and the traffic intensity from a [1, 2.5] uniform distribution while the relative profit margin for each order class was drawn from a [1, 5] triangular distribution for each problem instance, all regardless of the problem class.

The chosen parameters of the number of order classes and the maximum inventory capacity resulted in a certain range of maximum lead times, which is shown in table 4.1 as well.

The results for comparing the FCFS policy described above to the ϵ-optimal policy obtained by value iteration can be seen in table 4.2 and in figure 4.15.

problem class →	1	2	3
problem instances	100	100	100
average [%]	5.3	1.1	1.7
minimum [%]	0.0	0.0	0.0
maximum [%]	132.2	38.8	90.7
standard deviation [%]	19.4	4.4	9.2
running time simulation [sec.]	8.1	12.1	17.3
running time value iteration [sec.]	17.3	359.6	1,376.7

Table 4.2: Percentage deviations $\Delta^{\text{FCFS}-\text{opt}}$ of average rewards of the ϵ-optimal policy compared to the FCFS policy

100 problem instances were created for each problem class. Table 4.2 also shows the average running times of the procedures to determine the average reward of the FCFS policy and the ϵ-optimal average reward per period. The percentage deviation $\Delta^{\text{FCFS}-\text{opt}}$ of a certain problem instance within a problem class was calculated by

$$\Delta^{\text{FCFS}-\text{opt}} = \frac{\widehat{g}(\pi^\epsilon) - g(\pi^{\text{FCFS}})}{g(\pi^{\text{FCFS}})} \cdot 100\%$$

where $\widehat{g}(\pi^\epsilon)$ was the estimated average reward for the ϵ-optimal policy obtained by value iteration and $g(\pi^{\text{FCFS}})$ was the average reward of the FCFS policy.

Figure 4.15 shows that most percentage deviations lie in a [0%, 10%] or [0%, 20%] interval while there are some outliers in each problem class. The high maximum percentage deviations can be explained by the fact that sometimes the optimal maximum inventory level lies almost in the middle between zero and the maximum inventory capacity I^{max} while the FCFS policy chooses either a maximum inventory level of zero or $I^{\max}$. Thus, the simple heuristic that is used for the FCFS policy to determine the maximum inventory level is choosing an inventory level that is quite far away from the optimal inventory level which explains the high maximum percentage deviations in table 4.2.

Figure 4.15 also shows that most percentage deviations are near zero. This can be explained by the fact that the expected inventory holding cost of 0.505 is relatively high, see table 4.1. In the case of high inventory holding costs, the optimal maximum inventory level will be near zero which has several consequences.

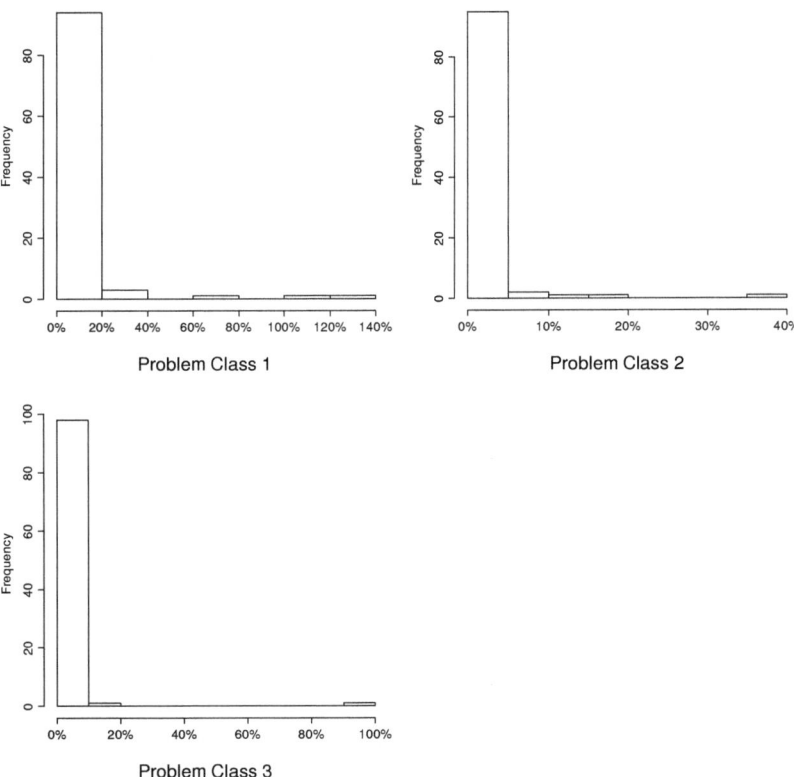

Figure 4.15: Histograms of the percentage deviations $\Delta^{\text{FCFS}-\text{opt}}$ of the ϵ-optimal policy compared to the FCFS policy

First, many order classes might not be able to be accepted any more at a maximum inventory level of zero because lead times that are below the order class usage are allowed, see the end of section 4.3.1. Furthermore, at a maximum inventory level of zero, less orders can be accepted at high capacity booking levels c than if the maximum inventory level would be higher. Overall one can say that at a maximum inventory level of zero the effective traffic intensity is reduced. At low traffic intensities, the difference in the average reward of the FCFS policy and the optimal average reward will be near zero, see also section 3.5.1.1. This explains why many percentage deviations $\Delta^{\text{FCFS}-\text{opt}}$ are near zero.

In the case of low inventory holding costs, a different picture emerges. 100 problem instances were created for each of the three problem classes and all problem instances had a low inventory holding cost of 0.01. Another 100 problem instances were created for each problem class, each with a high inventory holding cost of 1. The results can be seen in table 4.3 and figure 4.16.

problem class $\rightarrow$		1	2	3
problem instances	$(h = 0.01/h = 1)$	100/100	100/100	100/100
average [%]	$(h = 0.01/h = 1)$	5.9/1.2	3.4/1.0	5.5/0.2
minimum [%]	$(h = 0.01/h = 1)$	0.0/0.0	0.0/0.0	0.0/0.0
maximum [%]	$(h = 0.01/h = 1)$	29.7/18.3	26.6/23.6	37.8/6.6
standard deviation [%]	$(h = 0.01/h = 1)$	6.5/3.6	4.7/3.2	8.4/0.8

Table 4.3: $\Delta^{\text{FCFS}-\text{opt}}$ with a low and a high inventory holding cost h

At a low inventory holding cost, the maximum percentage deviations are not as extreme and the average percentage deviations are higher. This can be explained by the fact that at a low inventory holding cost, the optimal maximum inventory level will usually be equal to the maximum inventory capacity $I^{\max}$. Thus, the FCFS heuristic will usually find the optimal inventory level as well. Furthermore, if the optimal inventory level equals the maximum inventory capacity, the effective traffic intensity will be higher as more orders can be accepted for the optimal policy. Thus, the percentage differences $\Delta^{\text{FCFS}-\text{opt}}$ will be higher as well.

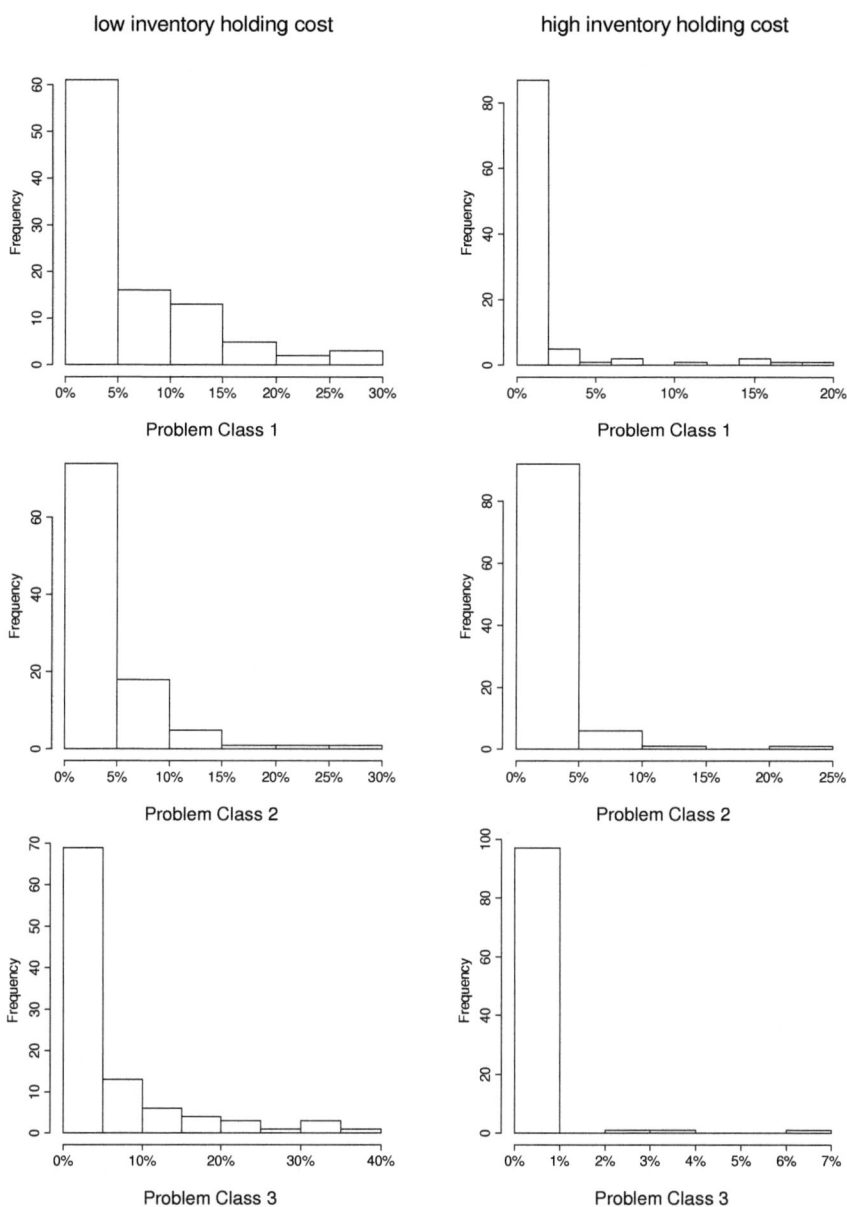

Figure 4.16: Histograms of the percentage deviations $\Delta^{\mathrm{FCFS-opt}}$ at a low and a high inventory holding cost

To illustrate these effects, the percentage deviations are also shown for high inventory holding costs in table 4.3 and figure 4.16. Here it is interesting to see that with a rising inventory capacity from problem class 1 through 3, the percentage deviations become lower. This is presumably because the high inventory holding costs will play a larger role with a larger maximum inventory capacity.

It is also interesting to investigate the effect of different traffic intensities on the percentage deviations $\Delta^{\text{FCFS-opt}}$. For this purpose, 100 problem instances were created for each problem class with a traffic intensity of $\rho = 1$ and 100 problem instances were created for each problem class with a traffic intensity of $\rho = 2.5$. The results can be seen in table 4.4 and the corresponding histograms in figure 4.17.

problem class $\rightarrow$		1	2	3
problem instances	$(\rho = 1/\rho = 2.5)$	100/100	100/100	100/100
average [%]	$(\rho = 1/\rho = 2.5)$	2.0/6.7	0.8/7.1	1.1/1.7
minimum [%]	$(\rho = 1/\rho = 2.5)$	0.0/0.0	0.0/0.0	0.0/0.0
maximum [%]	$(\rho = 1/\rho = 2.5)$	63.4/62.7	49.3/305.8	56.3/15.9
standard deviation [%]	$(\rho = 1/\rho = 2.5)$	7.9/13.4	5.3/31.0	6.9/3.4

Table 4.4: $\Delta^{\text{FCFS-opt}}$ with different traffic intensities

Table 4.4 shows that the average percentage deviations are generally higher for higher traffic intensities and lower for lower traffic intensities, similar to the basic model of revenue management of the previous chapter. It is interesting to see how low the percentage deviations are in problem class 3 for high traffic intensities compared to problem classes 1 and 2. These low percentage deviations might be explained by the fact that problem class 3 has the highest maximum inventory capacity of 50 units. Thus, the relatively high expected inventory holding cost of 0.505 might have the greatest influence on reducing the effective traffic intensity in this problem class.

When looking at table 4.4, one also notices the high maximum percentage deviations, especially the 305.8% for a high traffic intensity in problem class 2.

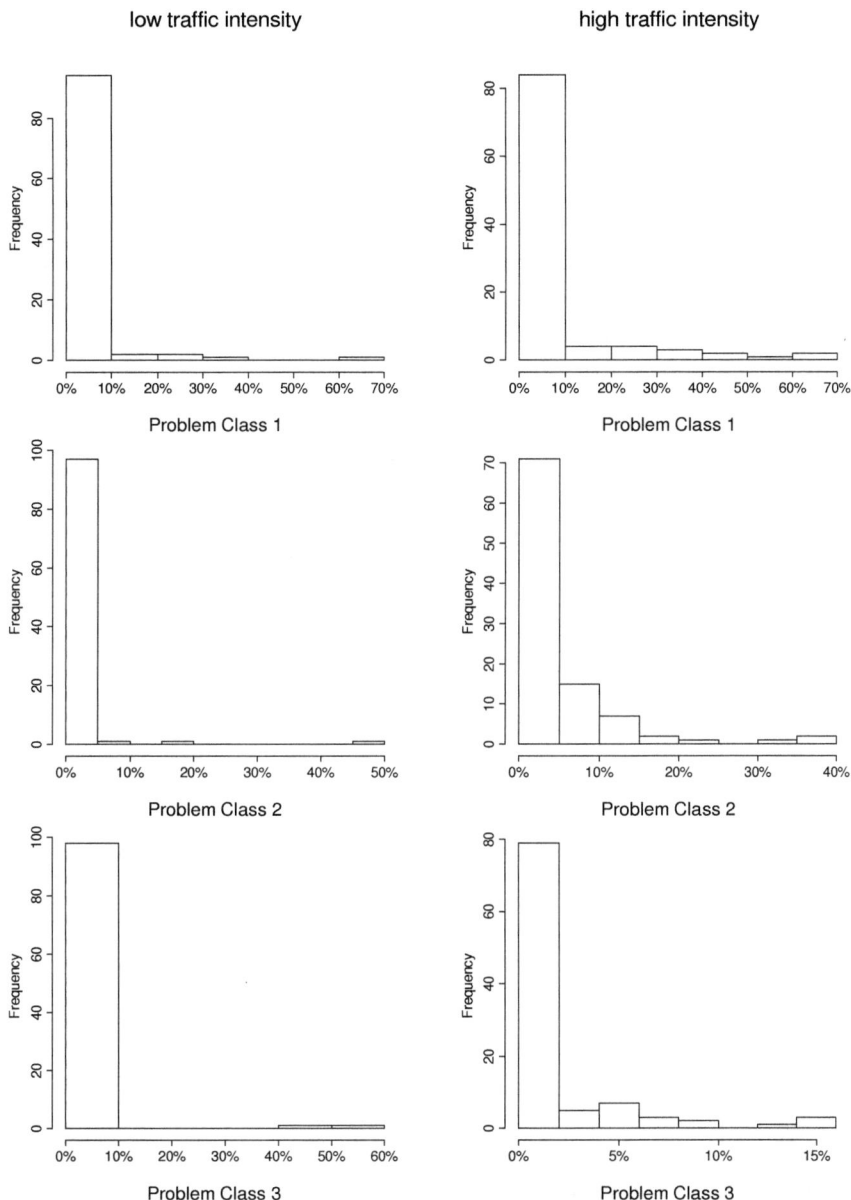

Figure 4.17: Histograms of the percentage deviations $\Delta^{\text{FCFS}-\text{opt}}$ at varying traffic intensities

These high maxima can again be explained by the fact that the maximum inventory level chosen by the FCFS policy is quite far away from the optimum maximum inventory level which usually lies in the middle between 0 and $I^{\max}$ for these problem instances. In order to conserve the explanatory power of the histogram with a high traffic intensity for problem class 2 in figure 4.17, the maximum value of 305.8% was not taken into account when producing this histogram.

Overall, one can conclude for this section that an optimal policy that uses revenue management can produce significant improvements over the FCFS policy with the simple heuristic to set the maximum inventory level, especially at a low inventory holding cost or at a high traffic intensity.

4.3.3   Comparing the Heuristic to an Optimal Procedure

In order to estimate the performance of the heuristic procedure which was described in section 4.2 the heuristic was compared to value iteration. The problem classes were the same as in section 4.3.2, see table 4.1.

The results of comparing both procedures are shown in table 4.5 and figure 4.18.

problem class →	1	2	3
problem instances	100	100	100
average [%]	1.7	0.4	0.2
minimum [%]	0.0	0.0	0.0
maximum [%]	114.0	16.6	6.8
standard deviation [%]	11.7	1.8	0.8
running time heuristic [sec.]	16.7	21.1	38.4
running time value iteration [sec.]	17.3	359.6	1,376.7

Table 4.5: Percentage deviations $\Delta^{\text{H}-\text{opt}}$ of average rewards of the ϵ-optimal policy compared to the heuristic policy

100 problem instances were created for each problem class. The running times show that the average running times of the heuristic procedure grow

much slower with respect to the problem size than the average running times of value iteration. The percentage deviation $\Delta^{\mathrm{H-opt}}$ of a certain problem instance was calculated by

$$\Delta^{\mathrm{H-opt}} = \frac{\widehat{g}(\pi^\epsilon) - g(\tilde{\pi})}{g(\tilde{\pi})} \cdot 100\%$$

where $\widehat{g}(\pi^\epsilon)$ was the estimated average reward for the ϵ-optimal policy obtained by value iteration and $g(\tilde{\pi})$ was the average reward obtained by the heuristic procedure.

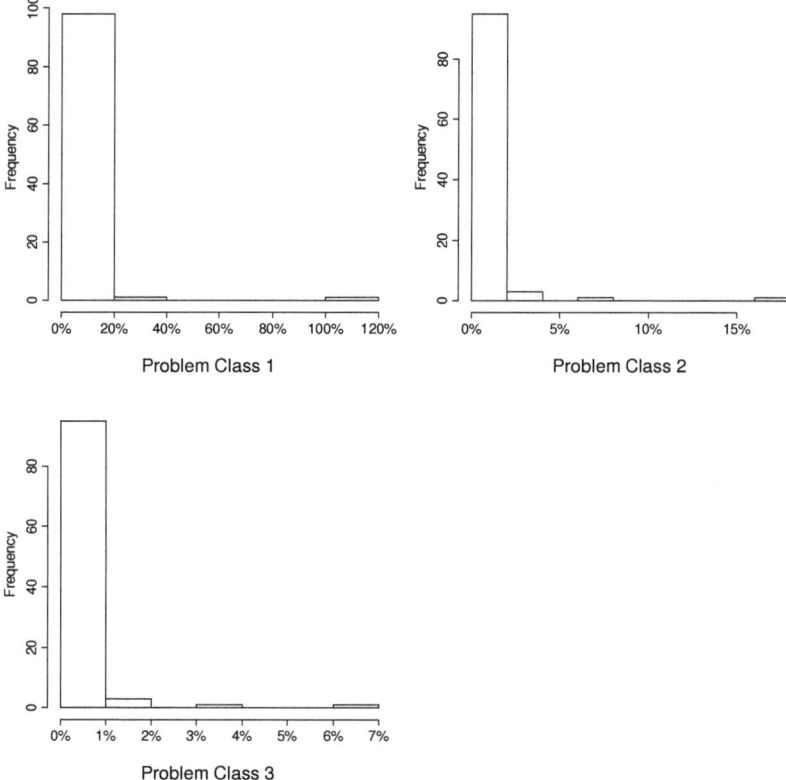

Figure 4.18: Histograms of the percentage deviations $\Delta^{\mathrm{H-opt}}$ of the ϵ-optimal policy compared to the heuristic policy

On average, the heuristic procedure performs between 1.7% for problem class 1 and 0.2% for problem class 3 worse than the ϵ-optimal procedure. The relatively high maximum percentage deviation Δ^{H-opt} of 114% for problem class 1 results from the fact that the average rewards are near zero. The average reward of the heuristic procedure is about 6.17E-02 monetary units while the average reward of the optimal procedure is about 1.32E-01 monetary units. Thus, the absolute difference is still relatively small with about 1.26E-01 monetary units. Overall, the heuristic procedure performs well.

The heuristic procedure was also compared to value iteration for low and high inventory holding costs traffic intensities. The results are shown in tables 4.6 and 4.7.

problem class →		1	2	3
problem instances	$(h = 0.01/h = 1)$	100/100	100/100	100/100
average [%]	$(h = 0.01/h = 1)$	1.4/0.3	1.0/0.4	1.2/0.1
minimum [%]	$(h = 0.01/h = 1)$	0.0/0.0	0.0/0.0	0.0/0.0
maximum [%]	$(h = 0.01/h = 1)$	7.9/5.5	7.2/10.5	12.4/6.6
standard deviation [%]	$(h = 0.01/h = 1)$	1.8/0.7	1.5/1.4	1.8/0.7

Table 4.6: Δ^{H-opt} with varying inventory holding costs h

Table 4.6 shows that the heuristic procedure performs between 1.2% and 1.4% worse than value iteration on average for low inventory holding costs and between 0.1% and 0.3% for high inventory holding costs.

problem class →		1	2	3
problem instances	$(\rho = 1/\rho = 2.5)$	100/100	100/100	100/100
average [%]	$(\rho = 1/\rho = 2.5)$	0.2/1.0	0.2/1.1	0.1/0.5
minimum [%]	$(\rho = 1/\rho = 2.5)$	0.0/0.0	0.0/0.0	0.0/0.0
maximum [%]	$(\rho = 1/\rho = 2.5)$	11.5/17.5	16.9/20.5	4.9/6.8
standard deviation [%]	$(\rho = 1/\rho = 2.5)$	1.2/2.4	1.7/3.1	0.6/1.1

Table 4.7: Δ^{H-opt} with varying traffic intensities ρ

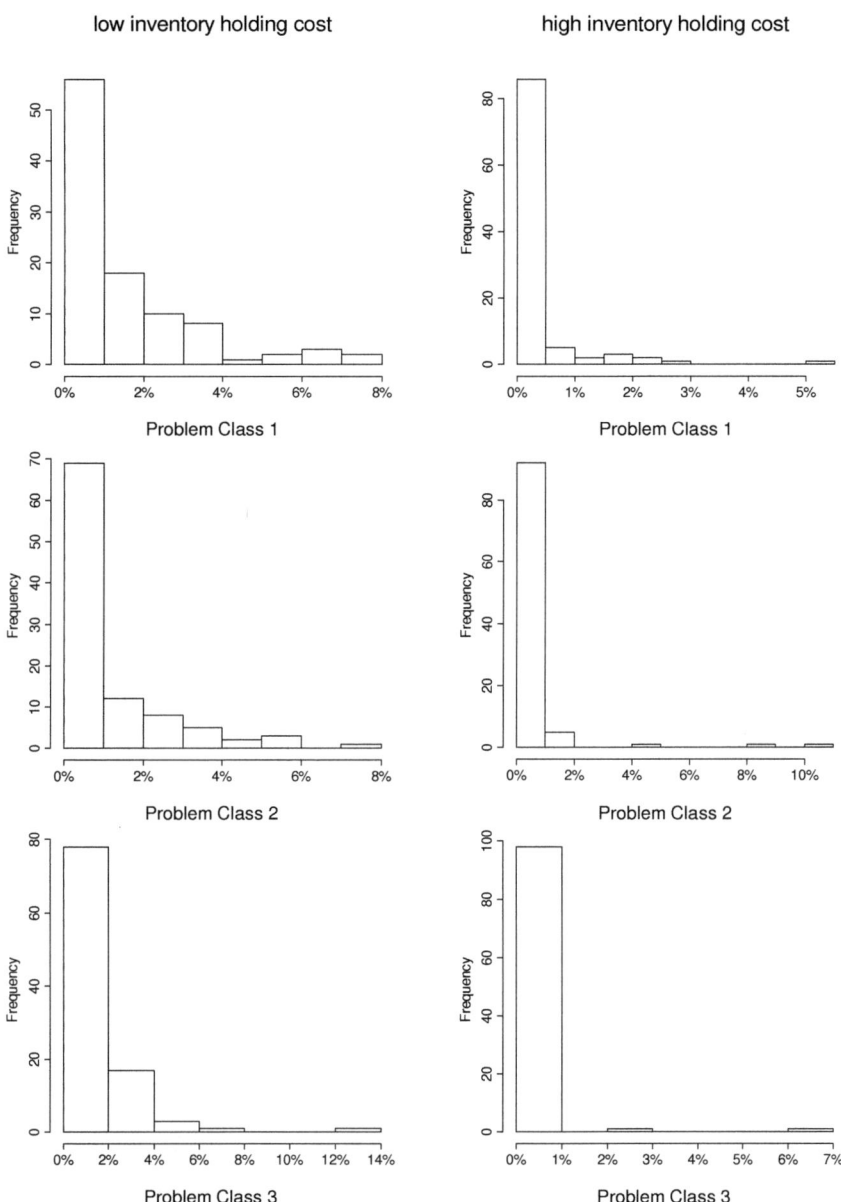

Figure 4.19: Histograms of the percentage deviations $\Delta^{\mathrm{H-opt}}$ at varying inventory holding costs

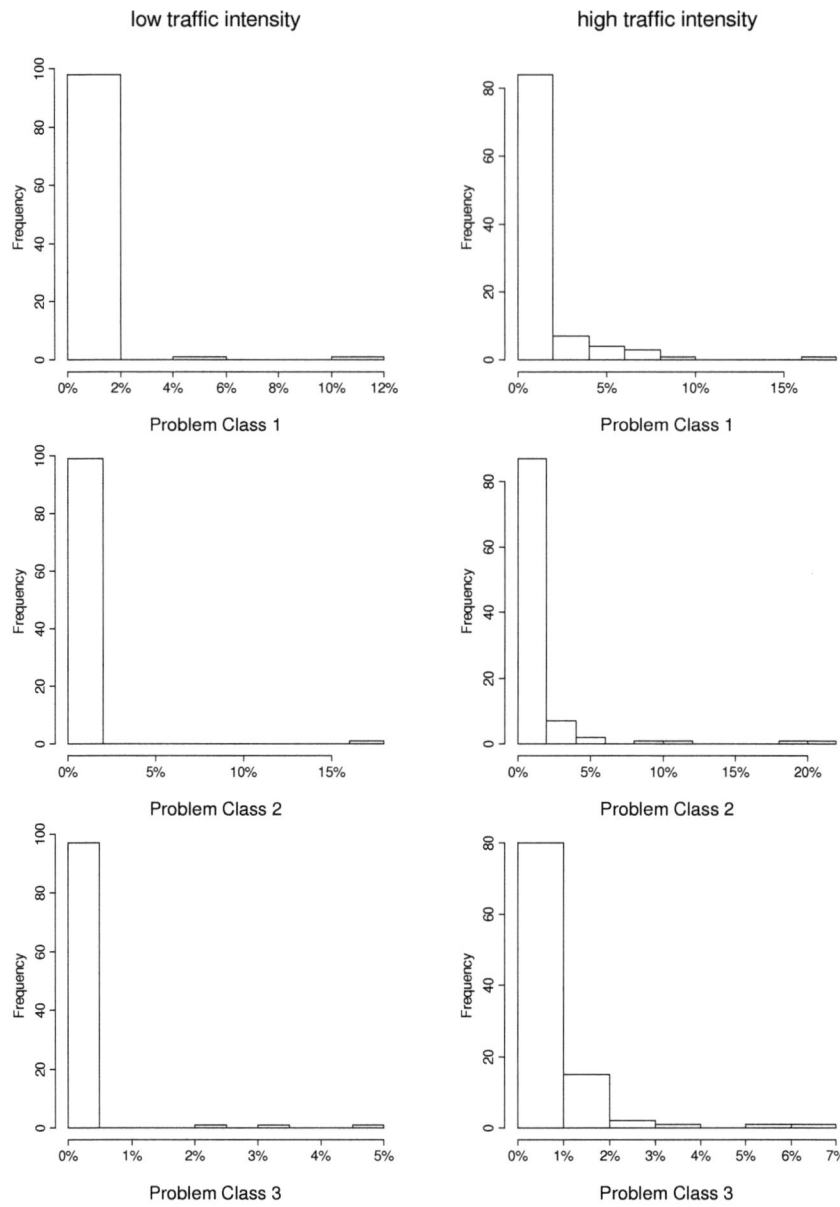

Figure 4.20: Histograms of the percentage deviations $\Delta^{\mathrm{H-opt}}$ at varying traffic intensities

Table 4.7 shows that the heuristic procedure performs between 0.1% and 0.2% worse than value iteration on average for low traffic intensities and between 0.5% and 1.1% for high traffic intensities. Overall, one can conclude that the heuristic procedure performs quite well.

This impression is substantiated by the histograms in figures 4.19 and 4.20 which give a more detailed picture of the distributions of the percentage deviations.

4.3.4 Comparing the Heuristic to a FCFS Policy

In order to measure the value of the heuristic procedure for large problem instances, it was compared to the FCFS policy that was described in section 4.3.2. Table 4.8 shows the two problem classes that were used to compare the heuristic procedure to a FCFS policy.

problem class →	4	5
number of states	500,000	1,000,000
number of order classes	[10, 50]	[10, 50]
maximum inventory capacity	100	100
inventory holding cost	[0.01, 1]	[0.01, 1]
relative profit margin	[1, 5]	[1, 5]
traffic intensity	[1, 2.5]	[1, 2.5]
maximum lead time	[97, 450]	[194, 900]

Table 4.8: Problem classes for comparing a FCFS policy to the heuristic policy

As in section 3.5.3, two problem classes with 500,000 and 1,000,000 states were used as large problem classes. The number of instances in each problem class was set to 100. The number of order classes in each problem instance was drawn from a uniform [10, 50] distribution while the maximum inventory capacity $I^{\max}$ was set to 100. The inventory holding cost of each problem instance was drawn from a [0.01, 1] uniform distribution and the relative profit margin of each order class within a problem instance was drawn from a left-triangular [1, 5] distribution. The traffic intensity for each problem instance was drawn from a [1, 2.5] uniform distribution. The maximum lead times in table 4.8 result from the number of order classes that has been drawn for a certain problem instance and equation (4.1).

Table 4.8 also shows the average running times for obtaining the average reward of the FCFS policy and for performing the heuristic procedure. The running times are significantly lower than the running times in section 3.5.3. This is because the variance in average rewards is lower for the inventory model compared to the average rewards of the basic model. The higher variance in average rewards for the basic model results in more simulation runs for the basic model until the maximum relative error $\gamma = 0.5\%$ can be met.

Table 4.9 and figure 4.21 show the results of comparing the heuristic procedure to the FCFS policy. The percentage deviations $\Delta^{\text{FCFS-H}}$ were calculated by

$$\Delta^{\text{FCFS-H}} = \frac{g(\tilde{\pi}) - g(\pi^{\text{FCFS}})}{g(\pi^{\text{FCFS}})} \cdot 100\%$$

where $g(\tilde{\pi})$ and $g(\pi^{\text{FCFS}})$ were the average rewards obtained by simulation.

problem class $\rightarrow$	4	5
problem instances	100	100
average [%]	2.3	0.5
minimum [%]	0.0	0.0
maximum [%]	121.0	15.2
standard deviation [%]	13.2	2.1
running time FCFS [sec.]	30.7	40.4
running time heuristic [sec.]	77.8	89.6

Table 4.9: Percentage deviations $\Delta^{\text{FCFS-H}}$ of average rewards of the optimal policy compared to the FCFS policy

For problem class 4 the average percentage deviation is 2.3% and for problem class 5 the average percentage deviation is 0.5%. The relatively high maximum percentage deviation for problem class 4 shows the potential usefulness of the heuristic procedure for large problem instances.

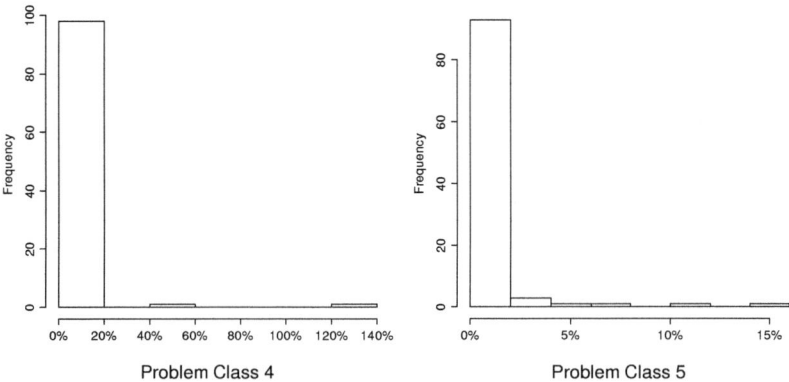

Figure 4.21: Histograms of the percentage deviations $\Delta^{\mathrm{FCFS-H}}$ of the heuristic policy compared to the FCFS policy

The heuristic procedure was also compared to the FCFS policy for low and high inventory holding costs. The results can be seen in table 4.10.

problem class →		4	5
problem instances	$(h = 0.01/h = 1)$	100/100	100/100
average [%]	$(h = 0.01/h = 1)$	2.9/0.1	2.5/0.3
minimum [%]	$(h = 0.01/h = 1)$	0.0/0.0	0.0/0.0
maximum [%]	$(h = 0.01/h = 1)$	35.9/1.8	48.3/6.4
standard deviation [%]	$(h = 0.01/h = 1)$	5.1/0.2	5.4/1.1

Table 4.10: $\Delta^{\mathrm{FCFS-H}}$ with a low and a high inventory holding cost h

It can be seen that for low inventory holding costs the percentage deviations lie above 2% on average while for high inventory holding costs the percentage deviations are rather low. Even then, the maximum percentage deviation of 6.4% in problem class 5 is remarkable.

Table 4.11 shows the results for low and high traffic intensities. At a traffic intensity of 1 the heuristic was not able to outperform the FCFS policy in even a single problem instance of problem class 4. Nevertheless, table 4.11

shows that substantial improvements are possible, especially in problem class 5.

problem class →		4	5
problem instances	$(\rho = 1/\rho = 2.5)$	100/100	100/100
average [%]	$(\rho = 1/\rho = 2.5)$	0.0/0.5	0.3/0.8
minimum [%]	$(\rho = 1/\rho = 2.5)$	0.0/0.0	0.0/0.0
maximum [%]	$(\rho = 1/\rho = 2.5)$	0.0/6.9	25.5/38.2
standard deviation [%]	$(\rho = 1/\rho = 2.5)$	0.0/1.3	2.5/3.9

Table 4.11: $\Delta^{\text{FCFS}-\text{H}}$ with varying traffic intensities ρ

The histograms in figures 4.22 and 4.23 show the distributions of the percentage deviations in more detail. Overall, one can conclude that the heuristic procedure can bring significant improvements over the FCFS policy for large problem instances.

Concluding the numerical tests for this chapter, it turned out that the percentage deviations $\Delta^{\text{H - opt}}$ can be quite high for small problem instances, but mainly when the average rewards are near zero which causes even small absolute deviations to result in large percentage deviations. Nevertheless, one should use an optimal procedure for small problem instances because the percentage deviations of the heuristic procedure from the optimal procedure can be significant even without factoring in the effect which results from average rewards being near zero. For large problem instances, optimal solution procedures can not be solved within a reasonable amount of time. Here, it turns out that the heuristic procedure is able to produce a significant value when compared to a FCFS policy and the heuristic procedure should thus be recommended for usage in an implementation with real-world problem instances.

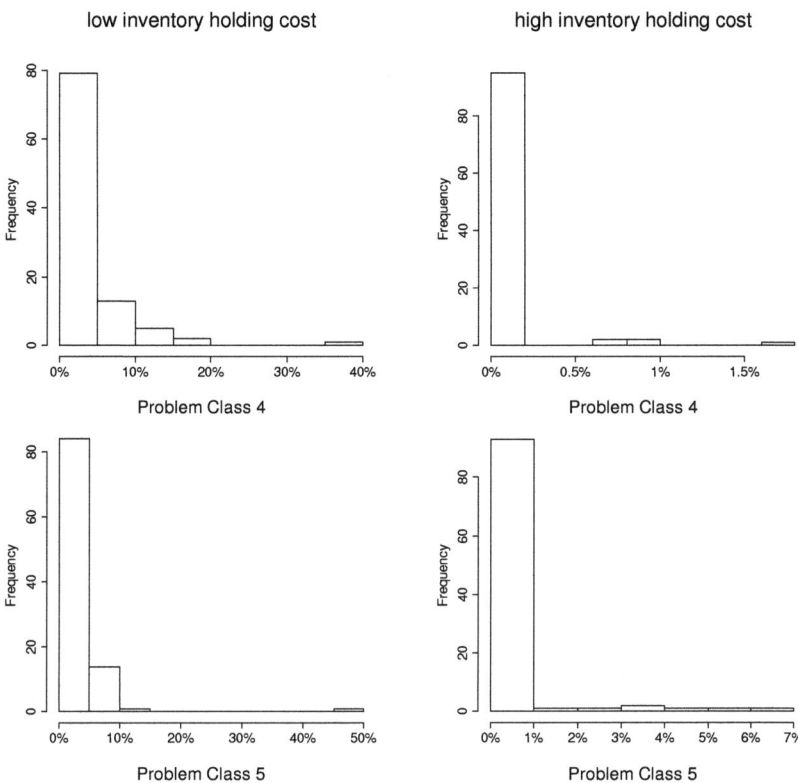

Figure 4.22: Histograms of the percentage deviations $\Delta^{\text{FCFS}-\text{H}}$ at low and high inventory holding costs

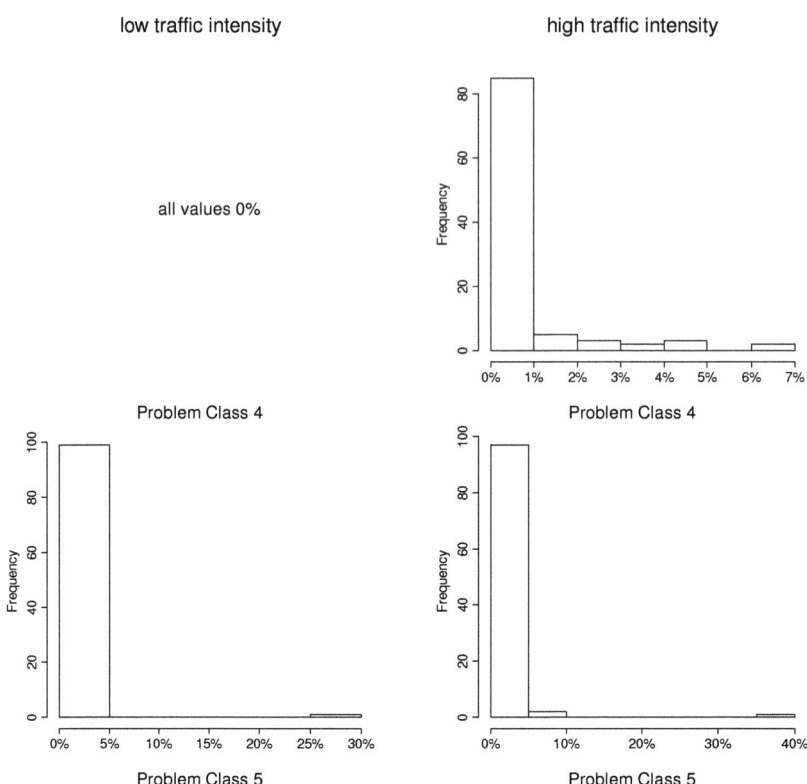

Figure 4.23: Histograms of the percentage deviations $\Delta^{\mathrm{FCFS-H}}$ at a low and a high traffic intensity

Chapter 5

Setup Times and Costs

5.1 Model

In this chapter, the basic model is extended by sequence-dependent setup times and costs between different order classes.

5.1.1 Model Formulation

Again, the decision problem is modeled with a discrete-time, infinite-horizon Markov decision process with the optimization criterion of maximizing the long-term average reward per period. Each incoming order belongs to one of the order classes $n \in \{1, ..., N\}$. Orders of a specific order class n have a certain lead time of l_n periods, a processing time of u_n periods and a profit margin of m_n monetary units. In each discrete time period at most one order can arrive. The probability that an order of class n arrives at the beginning of each time period is given by p_n, $\sum_{n=1}^{N} p_n < 1$. It is possible that no order arrives in a period. This is modeled by the dummy order class 0, $p_0 = 1 - \sum_{n=1}^{N} p_n$. If an order of class n has been accepted and the last order that was accepted before belongs to order class m, a setup time t_{mn} and a setup cost o_{mn} are incurred, $t_{nn} = o_{nn} = 0 \forall n \in \{1, ..., N\}$.

The state of the system is observed at the beginning of each time period and is described by the three state variables:

- $n \in \{0, \ldots, N\}$ is the order class of the order that arrived at the beginning of the currently observed period

© Springer Fachmedien Wiesbaden GmbH, part of Springer Nature 2009
F. Defregger, *Revenue Management for Manufacturing Companies*, Edition KWV,
https://doi.org/10.1007/978-3-658-24037-0_5

- $c \in \{0, \ldots, (\max_n l_n) - 1\}$ is the number of periods the machine is still busy because of orders that have been accepted in the past and have not been completed yet

- $s \in \{1, \ldots, N\}$ is the order class of the last order that was accepted by the company, i.e. the setup state that the resource will occupy after all currently accepted orders have been processed

The state space is the set of all possible states (n, c, s) and is denoted by S. The number of states $|S|$ of a certain problem instance is given by

$$|S| = (N + 1)(\max_n l_n)N \tag{5.1}$$

In each state (n, c, s), the company can take two possible decisions D:

$$D[(n, c, s)] = \begin{cases} D1 := \text{"reject"}, \forall (n, c, s) \in S \\ D2 := \text{"accept"}, \forall (n, c, s) \in \{S : n > 0 \land c + u_n + t_{sn} \leq l_n\} \end{cases}$$

An incoming order can only be accepted if an order has in fact arrived and if the order can be finished within its lead time l_n while a possible setup change from order class s to order class n has to be taken into account. Any incoming order can also be rejected. If no order arrives, decision $D1$ is taken. Depending on the decision in state (n, c, s), the company receives a reward R :

$$R^{D1}[(n, c, s)] = 0, \qquad \forall (n, c, s) \in S$$
$$R^{D2}[(n, c, s)] = m_n - o_{sn}, \quad \forall (n, c, s) \in S$$

If an order has been rejected, no reward is received while if an order is accepted, the company receives the profit margin of the order which is decreased by a possible setup cost o_{sn}.

The transition probabilities P of the Markov decision process show which states can be reached from a state (n, c, s) once the decision to accept or reject an order has been taken.

$$P^{D1}[(n, c, s), (m, \max\{c - 1, 0\}, s)] = p_m, \forall (n, c, s) \in S, \forall m \in \{0, \ldots, N\}$$

If an order has been rejected, the number of periods c that the machine is still busy in order to complete all orders that have been accepted so far will be reduced by one period in the beginning of the next period. If an incoming order has been accepted, the capacity booking level c is increased accordingly:

$$P^{D2}[(n,c,s),(m,c+t_{sn}+u_n-1,n)] = \begin{cases} p_m, & \forall (n,c,s) \in S, m \in \{0,\ldots,N\} \\ 0, & \text{else} \end{cases}$$

All states, decisions, rewards and transition probabilities that we described above specify a discrete-time Markov decision process with an infinite time horizon.

In order to find the optimal decision for each state and thus the optimal policy and the optimal average reward per period, different solution procedures exist which depend on the type of the Markov decision process. Thus, the Markov decision process has to be classified before a solution procedure can be applied.

5.1.2   Model Classification

We will first show that the Markov decision process described above can be classified as multichain. A Markov decision process can be classified as multichain if any policy can be found that results in a Markov reward process with two or more irreducible classes, see Puterman (1994). For the Markov decision process described above such a policy can be found by accepting only orders in a state (n,c,s) if $n > 0 \wedge c + u_n + t_{sn} \le l_n$, as described above, and the additional condition that $n = s$. The additional condition specifies that orders are only accepted if no setup is incurred. With this policy, the setup state of the resource will never change and depends entirely on the setup state at the beginning of the first period of the infinite time horizon. Thus, depending on the initial setup state of the resource, the stochastic process will evolve into different irreducible classes and the Markov decision process can be classified as multichain.

Furthermore, a Markov decision process can be classified as communicating if for every pair of states $a, b \in S$ an arbitrary policy can be found under which a is accessible from b. To show that the Markov decision process is communicating, a policy can be found that results in all possible outcomes of the state variables n, c and s.

Order class n. With regards to the state variable n, the Markov decision process is communicating regardless of any policy because any order of class $n \in \{0, \ldots, N\}$ can arrive in every period.

Capacity booking level c. Under any policy the capacity booking level c can always decrease to 0 if for a very long number of periods no orders arrive which is possible because of $p_0 > 0$. On the other hand, there is a positive probability that the booking level c can reach its maximum if an order arrives in every period and all incoming orders are accepted. Thus, all possible capacity booking levels c can be reached by a FCFS policy which accepts all orders.

Setup state s. The policy to reach all setup states s consists of the FCFS policy as well. As an order of any order class n can arrive in every period, all setup states can be reached by the FCFS policy provided that no order class n has such large setup times t_{mn} that no orders of this class can be accepted for any system state $(m, c, s), m \neq n$. This condition will be considered in the numerical tests when individual problem instances are created.

Thus, we showed that there exists a policy by which all possible realizations of the state variables n, c and s can be attained and the Markov decision process can be classified as communicating.

A solution procedure for a multichain and communicating Markov decision process is the value iteration algorithm, provided that all optimal policies induce aperiodical transition matrices. We will show this condition for all possible policies. Consider the assumption that no order arrives for a large number of periods, so that c decreases to zero and the stochastic process resulting from any policy will remain in the states $(0, 0, s)$. Thus, under all policies there will be transitions from state $(0, 0, s)$ into itself which is equivalent to the transition matrix being aperiodic, see Kulkarni (1999).

In conclusion, the value iteration algorithm for the multichain and communicating Markov decision process can be used in order to find the optimal policy and maximum average reward per period. Because of high running times, the value iteration algorithm can not be reasonably applied to large problem instances, so we suggest the following heuristic procedure.

5.2   A Heuristic Procedure

The idea of the heuristic procedure is to reject orders depending on the order class and the current setup state. This rejection of orders is done in order to increase the average reward that can be obtained in comparison to a FCFS policy that accepts all orders of all order classes regardless of the setup state that the resource currently occupies.

In order to start rejecting orders, artificial order classes are created. An artificial order class is specified by two components: the class n of an order that arrives in any given period and the setup state s of the resource in this period. All possible combinations (n, s) constitute the set of all artificial order classes $a \in \{1, ..., A\}$. The number of artificial order classes is given by $A = (N + 1) N$.

Before the heuristic procedure starts rejecting orders, the artificial order classes are sorted ascendingly by the following criterion:

$$\frac{m_n - o_{sn}}{u_n + t_{sn}}$$

This criterion resembles a relative profit margin m_n / u_n that additionally considers the relevant setup cost o_{sn} and setup time t_{sn} if the order of class n is accepted while the resource occupies the setup state s. After the artificial order classes have been sorted by the above criterion, the heuristic tries to find the optimal number of artificial order classes $\tilde{\omega}$ that should be rejected in order to find the best possible average reward per period.

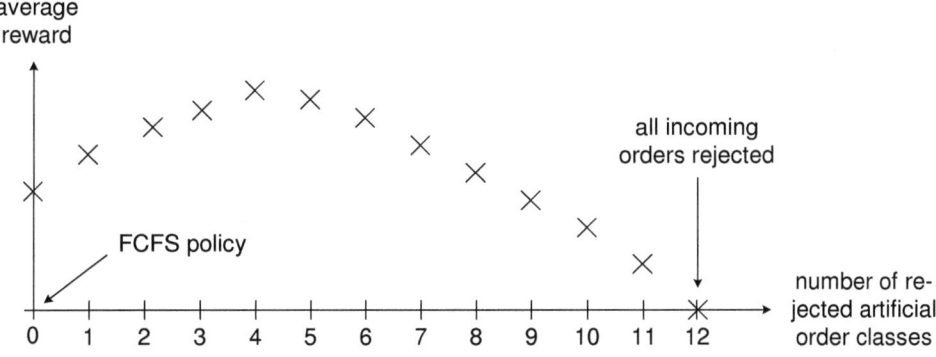

Figure 5.1: Example for the assumption that the average reward is a concave function of the number of rejected artificial order classes

This search process is guided by the assumption that the average reward

$g(\omega)$ is a concave function of the number of rejected artificial order classes ω. Figure 5.1 gives an example for a problem instance with $N = 3, A = 12$.

Figure 5.1 shows that if all artificial order classes are accepted, the average reward is equal to the average reward of a FCFS policy, if all artificial order classes are rejected, the average reward drops to zero. As this assumption is very similar to the assumption on how the average reward depends on the maximum inventory level in the previous chapter, the same algorithm was employed again and is outlined in algorithm 5.1.

Algorithm 5.1 is nearly identical to algorithm 4.1 of the previous chapter, the only difference is that instead of finding the best maximum inventory level $\tilde{I}$, algorithm 5.1 tries to find the best number of artificial order classes $\tilde{\omega}$ that should be rejected.

The idea of the search procedure is to continually update lower and upper bounds for the best number of rejected order classes $\tilde{\omega}$. The heuristic procedure starts by initializing the number of rejected artificial order classes that generates the highest average reward so far, $\tilde{\omega}$, a lower bound $\underline{\omega}$ and an upper bound $\overline{\omega}$ for $\tilde{\omega}$. Basically, the search procedure continually compares two policies ω_1 and ω_2 that are updated during the search process. The first two policies to be compared are the FCFS policy which accepts all orders and the policy that rejects all orders. Thus, ω_1 is initialized to zero artificial order classes that are rejected and ω_2 is initialized to all artificial order classes A that are rejected.

After that, a procedure is repeated which consists of the following steps. First, the lower and the upper bound and $\tilde{\omega}$, the best number of rejected artificial order classes found so far, are updated. In a second step, the number of rejected artificial order classes ω_1 and ω_2 that should be compared next are determined. To set ω_1 and ω_2, it is checked wether the updated bounds have roughly the same distance to $\tilde{\omega}$. If this is the case ω_1 and ω_2 are set depending on the current estimates of the average rewards $\hat{g}(\underline{\omega})$ and $\hat{g}(\overline{\omega})$ of the bounds $\underline{\omega}$ and $\overline{\omega}$. An example is given in figure 5.2.

Algorithm 5.1 Find the number of rejected artificial order classes $\tilde{\omega}$ that generates the highest average reward

---

$\tilde{\omega} \leftarrow 0, \underline{\omega} \leftarrow 0, \overline{\omega} \leftarrow A, \omega_1 \leftarrow 0, \omega_2 \leftarrow A$

compare ω_1 and ω_2 by simulation and estimate $\hat{g}(\omega_1)$ and $\hat{g}(\omega_2)$

$\hat{g}(\underline{\omega}) \leftarrow \hat{g}(\omega_1), \hat{g}(\overline{\omega}) \leftarrow \hat{g}(\omega_2)$

repeat

    if $\hat{g}(\omega_1) \geq \hat{g}(\omega_2)$ **then**

        $\tilde{\omega} \leftarrow \omega_1, \overline{\omega} \leftarrow \omega_2$

    else if $\hat{g}(\omega_2) > \hat{g}(\omega_1)$ **then**

        $\tilde{\omega} \leftarrow \omega_2, \underline{\omega} \leftarrow \omega_1$

    end if

    if $|(\overline{\omega} - \tilde{\omega}) - (\tilde{\omega} - \underline{\omega})| \leq 1$ **then** $\{\overline{\omega}$ and $\underline{\omega}$ have equal distance to $\tilde{\omega}\}$

        if $\hat{g}(\overline{\omega}) > \hat{g}(\underline{\omega})$ **then**

            $\omega_1 \leftarrow \tilde{\omega}, \omega_2 \leftarrow \tilde{\omega} + \lfloor(\overline{\omega} - \tilde{\omega})/2\rfloor$

        else $\{\hat{g}(\overline{\omega}) \leq \hat{g}(\underline{\omega})\}$

            $\omega_2 \leftarrow \tilde{\omega}, \omega_1 \leftarrow \tilde{\omega} - \lfloor(\tilde{\omega} - \underline{\omega})/2\rfloor$

        end if

    else $\{\overline{\omega}$ and $\underline{\omega}$ do not have equal distance to $\tilde{\omega}\}$

        if $\tilde{\omega} - \underline{\omega} < \overline{\omega} - \tilde{\omega}$ **then** $\{\tilde{\omega}$ is closer to $\underline{\omega}$ than to $\overline{\omega}\}$

            $\omega_1 \leftarrow \tilde{\omega}, \omega_2 \leftarrow \tilde{\omega} + \lfloor(\overline{\omega} - \tilde{\omega})/2\rfloor$

        else if $\overline{\omega} - \tilde{\omega} < \tilde{\omega} - \underline{\omega}$ **then** $\{\tilde{\omega}$ is closer to $\overline{\omega}$ than to $\underline{\omega}\}$

            $\omega_2 \leftarrow \tilde{\omega}, \omega_1 \leftarrow \tilde{\omega} - \lfloor(\tilde{\omega} - \underline{\omega})/2\rfloor$

        end if

    end if

    compare ω_1 and ω_2 by simulation and estimate $\hat{g}(\omega_1)$ and $\hat{g}(\omega_2)$

until $\omega_2 - \omega_1 \leq 1$

if $\hat{g}(\omega_1) \geq \hat{g}(\omega_2)$ **then**

    $\tilde{\omega} \leftarrow \omega_1$

else

    $\tilde{\omega} \leftarrow \omega_2$

end if

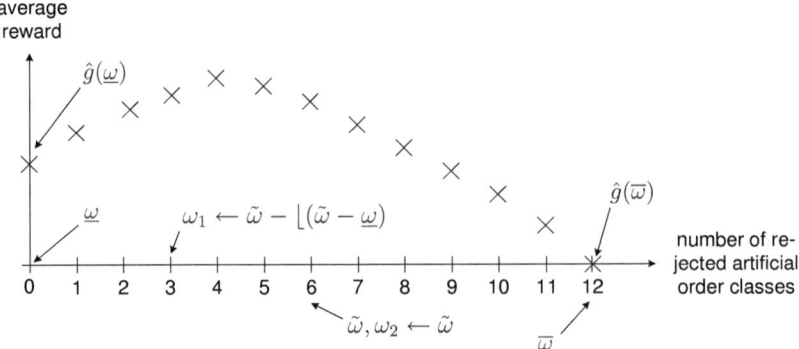

Figure 5.2: Setting ω_1 and ω_2 if $\tilde{\omega}$ has the same distance to $\underline{\omega}$ and $\overline{\omega}$ and $\hat{g}(\overline{\omega}) \leq \hat{g}(\underline{\omega})$

If the bounds $\underline{\omega}$ and $\overline{\omega}$ do not have the same distance to $\tilde{\omega}$, ω_1 and ω_2 are set depending on the distances of the bounds to $\tilde{\omega}$ which is illustrated in figure 5.3.

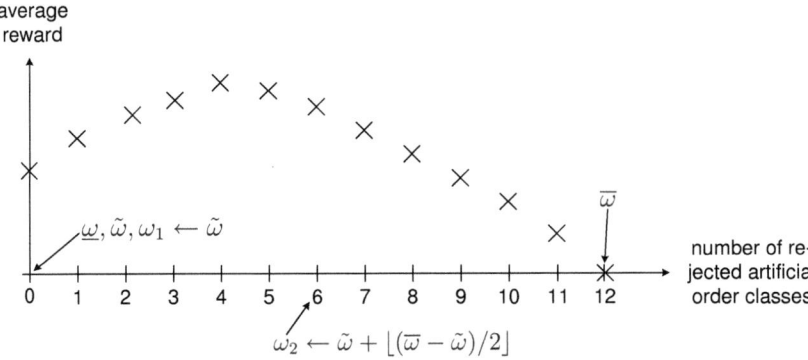

Figure 5.3: Setting ω_1 and ω_2 if $\tilde{\omega}$ does not have the same distance to $\underline{\omega}$ and $\overline{\omega}$ and $\tilde{\omega}$ is closer to $\underline{\omega}$ than to $\overline{\omega}$

Two policies ω_1 and ω_2 are compared by simulation the paired-t confidence interval approach, see Law and Kelton (2000). After $\tilde{\omega}$ has been determined, the average reward associated to the policy of rejecting the first $\tilde{\omega}$ artificial order classes is estimated by simulation with a maximum relative error of $\gamma = 0.5\%$ and a confidence level of 95%.

5.3 Numerical Results

5.3.1 Creating Problem Instances

When creating problem instances for the model with setups, controlling the traffic intensity ρ of a problem instance becomes more elaborate because the setup times have an influence on the traffic intensity as well. Higher setup times will cause a higher workload for the single resource than lower or no setup times. For the basic and for the inventory model, ρ is given by $\rho = \sum_{n=1}^{N} p_n\, u_n$. For the model with setup times and costs ρ can be approximated by $\tilde{\rho} = \sum_{n=1}^{N} p_n\, x_n$ where

$$x_n = u_n + \bar{t}_n \tag{5.2}$$

and where $\bar{t}_n$ is the average setup time into order class n,

$$\bar{t}_n = \frac{1}{N} \sum_{m=1}^{N} t_{mn} \tag{5.3}$$

In order to create problem instances with an approximate $\tilde{\rho}$ our idea was to directly draw x_n for each order class n from a uniform $[10, l^{\max}]$ distribution. The sum x_n should be drawn for each order class n so that the relation of the order class usage u_n to the average setup time into order class n, $\bar{t}_n$, could be controlled externally by a parameter r for all order classes. Once x_n had been drawn for a certain order class, u_n was given by

$$u_n = r x_n \tag{5.4}$$

and $\bar{t}_n$ was given by

$$\bar{t}_n = x_n - u_n$$

By introducing the parameter r, problem instances with higher or lower average setup times $\bar{t}_n$ in relation to the processing times u_n could be created.

After $\bar{t}_n$ had been determined, the individual setup times t_{mn} into order class n could be drawn randomly while fulfilling the following condition:

$$\sum_{m=1}^{N} t_{mn} = N\bar{t}_n \tag{5.5}$$

see equation (5.3).

But a problem arose when x_n was drawn to be $l^{\max}$ because of the following two restrictions regarding the setup times t_{mn} into order class n:

$$u_n + t_{mn} \le l^{\max} \forall m \in \{1, \ldots, N\} \tag{5.6}$$

$$t_{nn} = 0 \tag{5.7}$$

Restriction (5.6) is needed to keep the model a communicating Markov decision process, see section 5.1.2. Restrictions (5.6) and (5.7) can not be fulfilled simultaneously if x_n has been drawn to equal $l^{\max}$.

This can be seen by the fact that even if all setup times $t_{mn}, m \ne n$, would be drawn to their maximum $l^{\max} - u_n$, the desired average of the $t_{mn}, m \in \{1, \ldots, N\}$, $\bar{t}_n = l^{\max} - u_n$ can not be reached because $t_{nn} = 0$.

Because of this problem, we introduce the average $\bar{t}'_n$ of the setup times $t_{mn}, m \ne n$,

$$\bar{t}'_n = \frac{1}{N-1} \sum_{m=1}^{N} t_{mn} \tag{5.8}$$

From equations (5.3) and (5.8), $\bar{t}_n$ can be expressed in terms of $\bar{t}'_n$ by

$$\bar{t}_n = \frac{N-1}{N} \bar{t}'_n \tag{5.9}$$

Instead of $x_n = u_n + \bar{t}_n$ the sum x'_n is drawn from a $[10, l^{\max}]$ uniform distribution for every order class n where

$$x'_n = u_n + \bar{t}'_n \tag{5.10}$$

After x'_n has been drawn it is necessary to express u_n in terms of x'_n and the input parameter r where

$$r = \frac{u_n}{u_n + \bar{t}_n}, \tag{5.11}$$

see equation (5.4). In order to obtain the expression of u_n in terms of x'_n and r one first transforms equation (5.11):

$$u_n(1 - r) = r\bar{t}_n$$

Expressing $\bar{t}_n$ in terms of $\bar{t}'_n$ and replacing $\bar{t}'_n$ by $\bar{t}'_n = x'_n - u_n$, one obtains

$$u_n(1 - r) = r\frac{N - 1}{N}\left(x'_n - u_n\right)$$

see equations (5.9) and (5.10). Solving to u_n and simplifying, one finally obtains

$$u_n = \frac{x'_n}{\left(\dfrac{1}{r} - 1\right)\dfrac{N}{N - 1} + 1} \tag{5.12}$$

Thus, after x'_n has been drawn, u_n can be calculated by equation (5.12).

Once u_n has been calculated, $\bar{t}'_n$ can be calculated by $\bar{t}'_n = x'_n - u_n$ and $\bar{t}_n$ can be calculated from equation (5.9).

After $\bar{t}_n$ has been obtained, the individual setup times t_{mn} can be drawn randomly while fulfilling conditions (5.5) through (5.7) in a fashion similar to algorithm 3.1. A fourth condition is used when creating the individual setup times t_{mn} into order class n:

$$t_{mn} < 3\bar{t}_n, \forall m \in \{1, \ldots, N\}$$

This is to prevent the case that one individual setup time t_{ln} becomes too large compared to the other setup times $t_{mn}, m \neq l$.

The setup costs o_{mn} are obtained by first drawing the relative setup costs o_{mn} from a $[0.01, 1]$ uniform distribution where

$$o_{mn}^{\mathrm{rel}} = o_{mn}/t_{mn}$$

The setup costs o_{mn} can then be calculated by $o_{mn} = o_{mn}^{\mathrm{rel}} t_{mn}$.

After the approximate traffic intensity of order class n, $\tilde{\rho}_n$, has been obtained using algorithm 3.1 and equation (3.3), the arrival probability of order class n is given by $p_n = \tilde{\rho}_n/(u_n + \bar{t}_n)$.

5.3.2   Comparing the Optimal Policy to a FCFS Policy

In order to investigate the potential of revenue management for the model with setup times and costs, the ϵ-optimal average reward obtained by value iteration was compared to the average reward of a FCFS policy, where ϵ and the maximum relative error γ were set to 0.5%. Under the FCFS policy, all orders were accepted as long as their lead times can be met and as long their profit margin is not smaller than the setup cost to fulfill the order. Numerical tests were performed for three problem classes which are outlined in table 5.1.

problem class $\rightarrow$	1	2	3
number of states	10,000	50,000	100,000
number of order classes	[5, 10]	[5, 20]	[5, 30]
relative setup cost	[0.01, 1]	[0.01, 1]	[0.01, 1]
relative profit margin	[1, 5]	[1, 5]	[1, 5]
approximate traffic intensity	[1, 2.5]	[1, 2.5]	[1, 2.5]
ratio setup times	[0.5, 0.9]	[0.5, 0.9]	[0.5, 0.9]
maximum lead time	[91, 333]	[119, 1667]	[108, 3333]

Table 5.1: Problem classes for comparing FCFS policies to ϵ-optimal policies

The number of order classes for each problem instance of a certain problem class was drawn from a uniform distribution whose parameters are given in table 5.1. The relative setup cost from a certain order class to all other order classes of a problem instance was drawn from a $[0.01, 1]$ uniform distribution while the relative profit margin of each order class was drawn from a $[1, 5]$ left triangular distribution. The approximate traffic intensity $\tilde{\rho}$ for each problem instance was drawn from a $[1, 2.5]$ uniform distribution while the parameter r to determine the average length of the setup times was drawn from a $[0.5, 0.9]$ uniform distribution for each problem instance within a certain problem class. The maximum lead times given in table 5.1 result from the number of order classes drawn for a certain problem instance and equation (5.1) in section 5.1.1. All calculations in this chapter were done on a desktop PC with a 3 GHz Pentium processor and 1 GB RAM, unlike to the numerical tests in chapters 3 and 4.

The results for comparing the ϵ-optimal average reward to the FCFS average reward are shown in table 5.2 and figure 5.4.

problem class →	1	2	3
problem instances	100	100	100
average [%]	8.9	8.1	8.2
minimum [%]	0.0	0.0	0.0
maximum [%]	42.9	42.6	30.7
standard deviation [%]	8.2	8.2	7.1
running time simulation [sec.]	2.5	3.6	8.1
running time value iteration [sec.]	2.2	29.9	111.9

Table 5.2: Percentage deviations $\Delta^{\text{FCFS}-\text{opt}}$ of average rewards of the ϵ-optimal policy compared to the FCFS policy

The percentage deviation $\Delta^{\text{FCFS}-\text{opt}}$ of a certain problem instance within a problem class was calculated by

$$\Delta^{\text{FCFS}-\text{opt}} = \frac{\widehat{g}(\pi^\epsilon) - g(\pi^{\text{FCFS}})}{g(\pi^{\text{FCFS}})} \cdot 100\%$$

where $\widehat{g}(\pi^\epsilon)$ was the estimated average reward for the ϵ-optimal policy obtained by value iteration and $g(\pi^{\text{FCFS}})$ was the average reward of the FCFS policy.

For each problem class, 100 problem instances were drawn randomly according to the distributions shown in table 5.1 and as described in section 5.3.1. Table 5.2 also shows the average running times for obtaining the average reward of the FCFS policy and for obtaining the optimal average reward.

Table 5.2 shows that on average, the optimal policy outperformed the FCFS policy by between 8% and 9%. This shows that using revenue management does indeed have a promising potential for the model with setup times and costs.

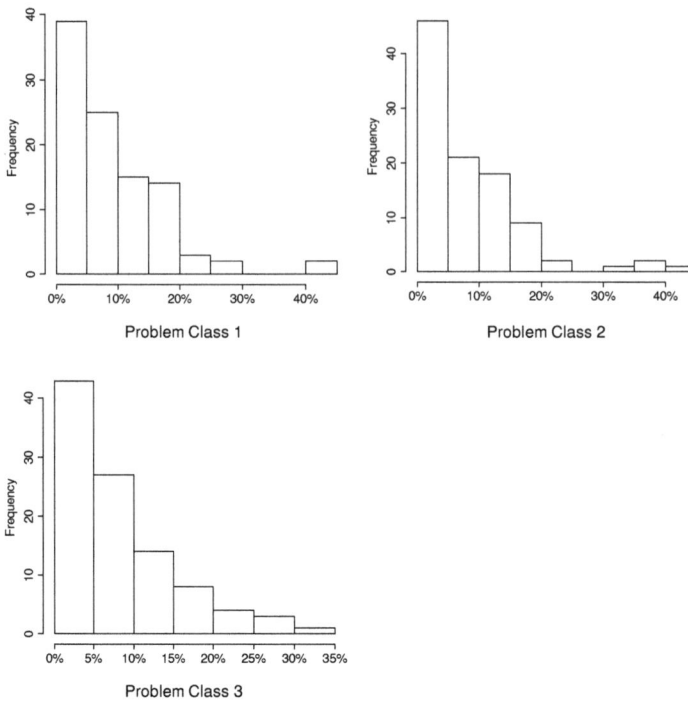

Figure 5.4: Histograms of the percentage deviations $\Delta^{\mathrm{FCFS-opt}}$ of the optimal policy compared to the FCFS policy

problem class $\rightarrow$		1	2	3
problem instances	$(r = 0.9/r = 0.5)$	100/100	100/100	100/100
average [%]	$(r = 0.9/r = 0.5)$	4.6/9.9	4.1/10.1	4.8/9.2
minimum [%]	$(r = 0.9/r = 0.5)$	0.0/0.0	0.0/0.0	0.0/0.0
maximum [%]	$(r = 0.9/r = 0.5)$	27.7/45.6	34.7/47.1	25.4/53.1
std. dev. [%]	$(r = 0.9/r = 0.5)$	5.3/7.9	4.7/8.4	4.5/8.2

Table 5.3: $\Delta^{\mathrm{FCFS-opt}}$ with low $(r = 0.9)$ and high $(r = 0.5)$ setup times

The potential of using revenue management instead of a FCFS policy was also investigated for varying setup times and traffic intensities. The results for varying setup times are shown in table 5.3 and figure 5.5.

For a reminder of the relationship between r and the length of the setup times, see equations (5.2) and (5.4). Table 5.3 shows that the potential for revenue management is higher when setup times are high. Overall, the improvements of the optimal average reward obtained by value iteration are substantial.

The potential of revenue management was also studied for different approximate traffic intensities $\tilde{\rho}$. The results are shown in table 5.4 and figure 5.6.

problem class $\rightarrow$		1	2	3
problem instances	$(\tilde{\rho}=1/\tilde{\rho}=2.5)$	100/100	100/100	100/100
average [%]	$(\tilde{\rho}=1/\tilde{\rho}=2.5)$	2.5/16.4	2.2/14.8	2.3/14.4
minimum [%]	$(\tilde{\rho}=1/\tilde{\rho}=2.5)$	0.0/0.7	0.0/0.0	0.0/0.0
maximum [%]	$(\tilde{\rho}=1/\tilde{\rho}=2.5)$	17.7/102.9	14.4/48.7	11.7/49.6
std. dev. [%]	$(\tilde{\rho}=1/\tilde{\rho}=2.5)$	3.5/15.3	2.8/10.1	2.4/10.1

Table 5.4: $\Delta^{\text{FCFS}-\text{opt}}$ with different approximate traffic intensities $\tilde{\rho}$

Table 5.4 shows that the optimal policy outperforms the FCFS policy even for an approximate traffic intensity of $\tilde{\rho}=1$. This indicates that $\tilde{\rho}$ is indeed an approximation of the traffic intensity and underestimates the true traffic intensity because one would expect no significant improvement of the optimal policy compared to the FCFS policy if the true traffic intensity was $\rho=1$. Here, the true traffic intensity is larger than 1 because there are significant improvements of the optimal policy compared to the FCFS policy.

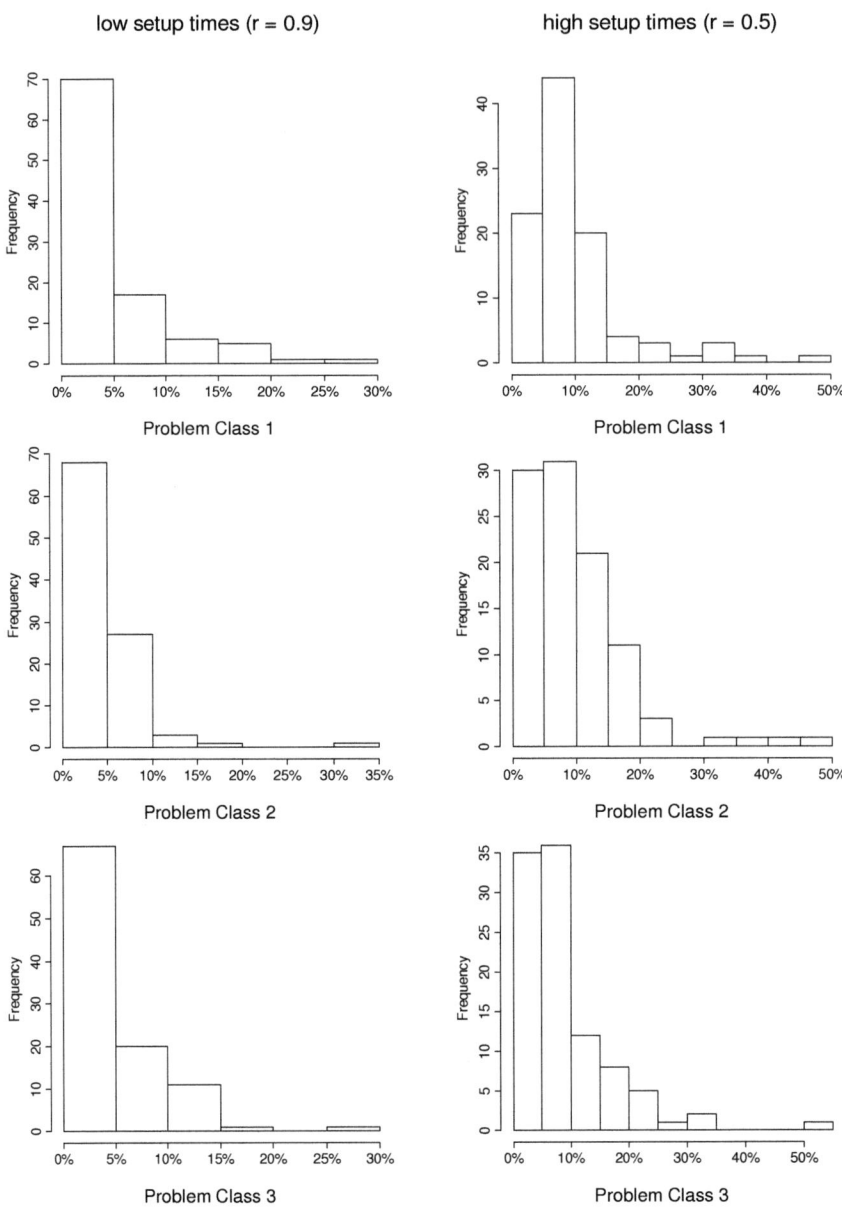

Figure 5.5: Histograms of the percentage deviations $\Delta^{\mathrm{FCFS-opt}}$ with low and high setup times

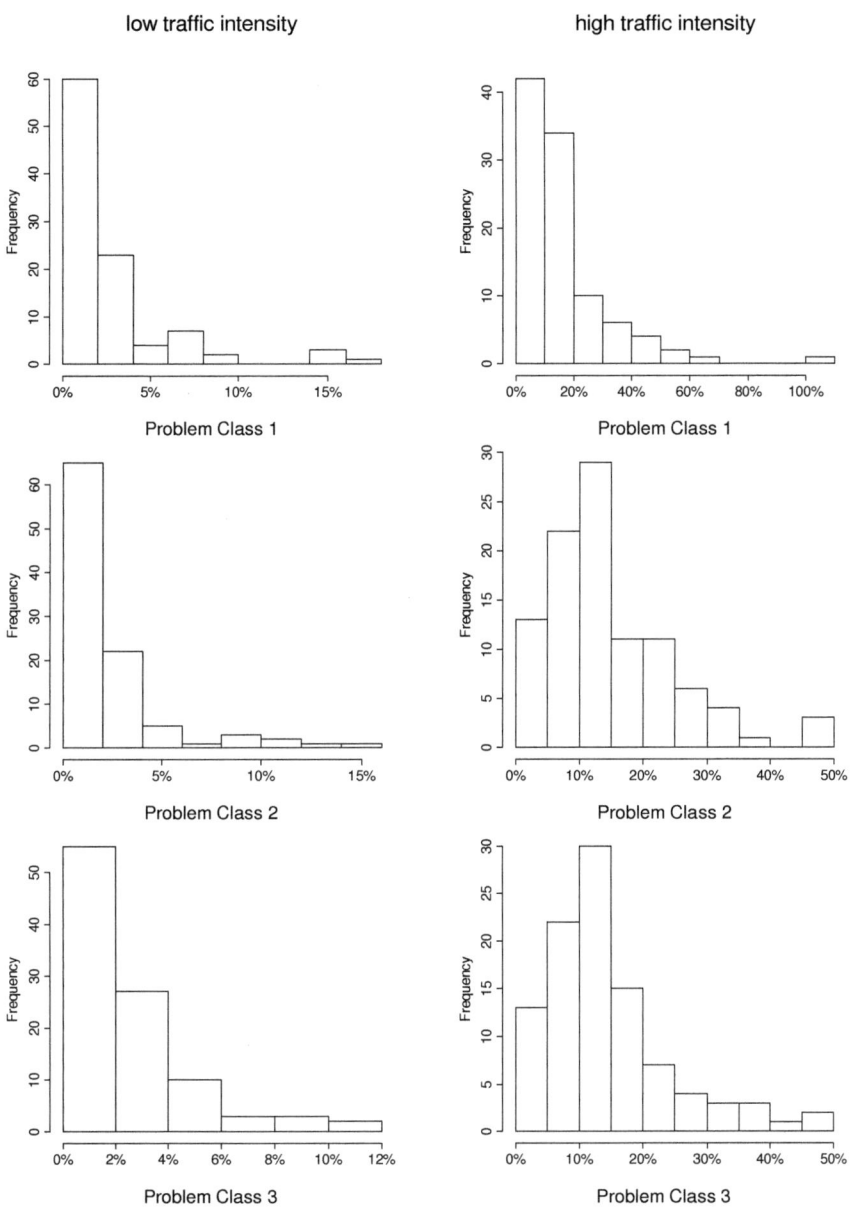

Figure 5.6: Histograms of the percentage deviations $\Delta^{\text{FCFS}-\text{opt}}$ at varying approximate traffic intensities $\tilde{\rho}$

Overall, table 5.4 shows that using revenue management offers significant improvements versus a simple FCFS policy. One can conclude for this section that using revenue management instead of a FCFS policy allows for significant improvements of the average reward per period when setup times and costs are present.

5.3.3   Comparing the Heuristic to an Optimal Procedure

In order to investigate the performance of the heuristic procedure that was proposed in section 5.2 it was compared to the value iteration algorithm which is an optimal procedure. The problem classes that were used to perform the comparison were the same as in section 5.3.2, see table 5.1. The results of comparing the heuristic procedure to the optimal procedure are shown in table 5.5 and figure 5.7.

problem class →	1	2	3
problem instances	100	100	100
average [%]	1.1	1.0	1.0
minimum [%]	0.0	0.0	0.0
maximum [%]	16.0	8.6	9.8
standard deviation [%]	2.3	1.7	1.5
running time heuristic [sec.]	10.3	12.3	41.2
running time value iteration [sec.]	2.2	29.9	111.9

Table 5.5: Percentage deviations $\Delta^{\text{H}-\text{opt}}$ of average rewards of the optimal policy compared to the heuristic policy

The percentage deviation $\Delta^{\text{H}-\text{opt}}$ of a certain problem instance was calculated by

$$\Delta^{\text{H}-\text{opt}} = \frac{\widehat{g}(\pi^\epsilon) - g(\tilde{\pi})}{g(\tilde{\pi})} \cdot 100\%$$

where $\widehat{g}(\pi^\epsilon)$ was the estimated average reward for the ϵ-optimal policy obtained by value iteration and $g(\tilde{\pi})$ was the average reward obtained by the heuristic procedure.

Table 5.5 shows that on average, the heuristic procedure performs about
1% worse than the optimal procedure. Although there are some significant
maxima, the histograms in figure 5.7 show that most percentage deviations
lie in the $[0\%, 2\%]$ and respectively the $[0\%, 1\%]$ intervals.

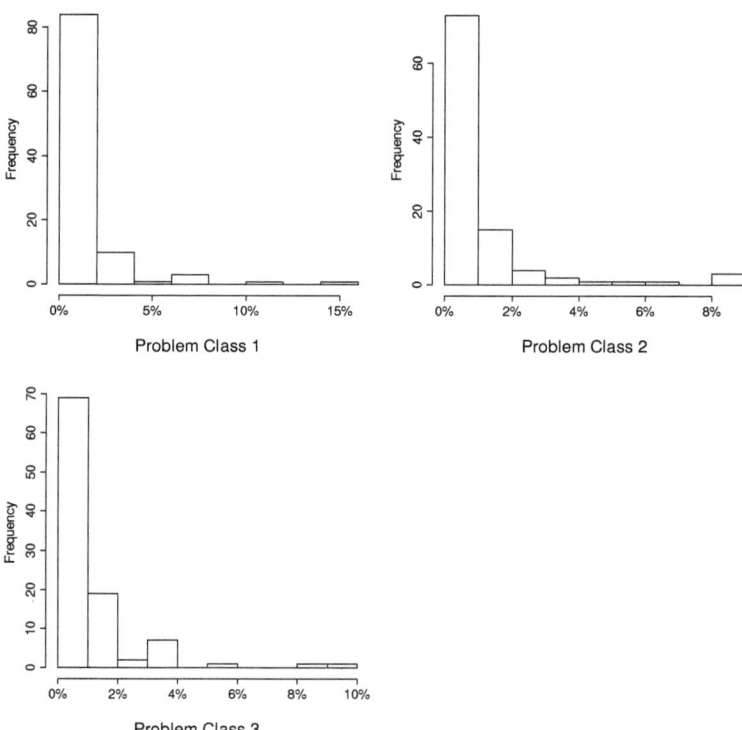

Figure 5.7: Histograms of the percentage deviations $\Delta^{\mathrm{H-opt}}$ of the optimal
policy compared to the heuristic policy

The heuristic procedure was also compared to the optimal procedure with
regards to differing setup times and approximate traffic intensities.

problem class →		1	2	3
problem instances	$(r = 0.9/r = 0.5)$	100/100	100/100	100/100
average [%]	$(r = 0.9/r = 0.5)$	0.2/2.5	0.2/2.2	0.2/1.7
minimum [%]	$(r = 0.9/r = 0.5)$	0.0/0.0	0.0/0.0	0.0/0.0
maximum [%]	$(r = 0.9/r = 0.5)$	3.0/27.3	1.2/12.9	2.2/14.4
standard deviation [%]	$(r = 0.9/r = 0.5)$	0.4/4.4	0.2/2.4	0.3/2.3

Table 5.6: $\Delta^{\mathrm{H-opt}}$ with low $(r = 0.9)$ and high $(r = 0.5)$ setup times

problem class →		1	2	3
problem instances	$(\tilde{\rho} = 1/\tilde{\rho} = 2.5)$	100/100	100/100	100/100
average [%]	$(\tilde{\rho} = 1/\tilde{\rho} = 2.5)$	0.5/2.0	0.3/1.9	0.2/2.5
minimum [%]	$(\tilde{\rho} = 1/\tilde{\rho} = 2.5)$	0.0/0.0	0.0/0.0	0.0/0.0
maximum [%]	$(\tilde{\rho} = 1/\tilde{\rho} = 2.5)$	12.3/20.2	2.3/15.9	3.4/15.8
standard deviation [%]	$(\tilde{\rho} = 1/\tilde{\rho} = 2.5)$	1.4/2.3	0.4/2.4	0.5/2.9

Table 5.7: $\Delta^{\mathrm{H-opt}}$ with different approximate traffic intensities $\tilde{\rho}$

The results are shown in table 5.6 and table 5.7. Table 5.6 shows that the heuristic procedure performs almost optimal when setup times are low. When setup times are high, the heuristic performs between 1.7% and 2.5% worse than value iteration. For different traffic intensities, a similar picture emerges. Figure 5.7 shows that the heuristic procedure performs between 0.2% and 0.5% on average worse than value iteration for an approximate traffic intensity of 1. For high traffic intensities, the heuristic procedure on average performs between 1.9% and 2.5% worse than value iteration.

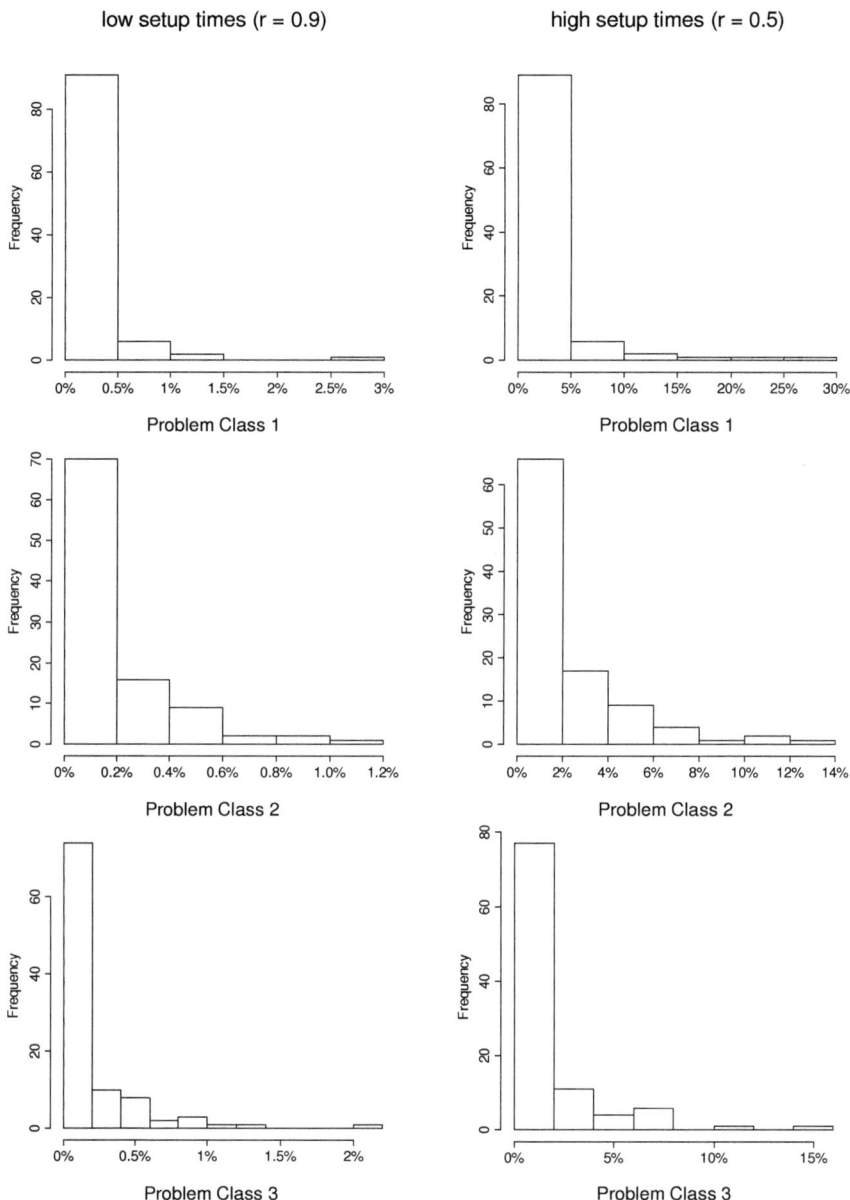

Figure 5.8: Histograms of the percentage deviations $\Delta^{\mathrm{H-opt}}$ with low and high setup times

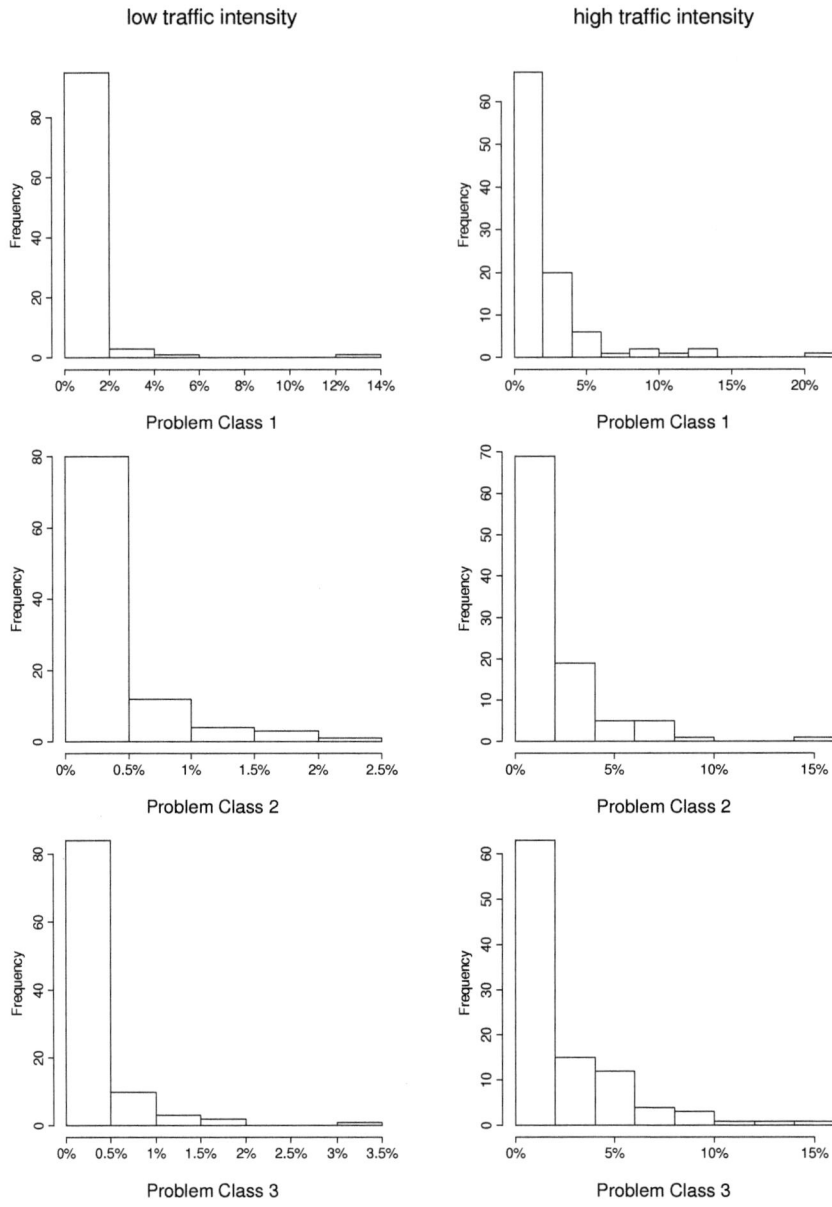

Figure 5.9: Histograms of the percentage deviations $\Delta^{\mathrm{H-opt}}$ at varying traffic intensities

5.3.4   Comparing the Heuristic to a FCFS Policy

In order to investigate the performance of the heuristic procedure for large problem instances it was compared to a FCFS policy which accepts all orders as long as their profit margin exceed the setup costs which have to be paid in order to accept the order. For this purpose, two more problem classes were defined which are described in table 5.8.

problem class $\rightarrow$	4	5
number of states	500,000	1,000,000
number of order classes	$[10, 50]$	$[10, 50]$
relative setup cost	$[0.01, 1]$	$[0.01, 1]$
relative profit margin	$[1, 5]$	$[1, 5]$
approximate traffic intensity	$[1, 2.5]$	$[1, 2.5]$
ratio setup times	$[0.5, 0.9]$	$[0.5, 0.9]$
maximum lead time	$[196, 4545]$	$[392, 9091]$

Table 5.8: Problem classes for comparing a FCFS policy to the heuristic policy

The number of order classes was drawn from a $[10, 50]$ uniform distribution for both problem classes and the relative setup cost was drawn from a $[0.01, 1]$ uniform distribution for every setup possible in each problem instance. The relative profit margin was drawn from a $[1, 5]$ left triangular distribution for every order class in every problem instance. The parameter r for the setup times was drawn from a $[0.5, 0.9]$ uniform distribution for every problem instance. The maximum lead times given in table 5.8 result from the number of order classes that was drawn for a certain problem instance and equation (5.1) in section 5.1.1.

The results of comparing the heuristic procedure to the FCFS policy for large problem instances can be seen in table 5.9.

problem class $\rightarrow$	4	5
problem instances	100	100
average [%]	7.5	5.7
minimum [%]	0.0	0.0
maximum [%]	37.1	32.7
standard deviation [%]	7.3	5.7
running time FCFS [sec.]	10.0	17.3
running time heuristic [sec.]	83.7	108.8

Table 5.9: Percentage deviations $\Delta^{\text{FCFS}-\text{H}}$ of average rewards of the optimal policy compared to the heuristic policy

It shows that on average, the heuristic procedure outperforms the FCFS policy by 7.5% for problem class 4 and 5.7% for problem class 5. The maximum percentage deviations show that using the heuristic instead of a FCFS policy can be indeed quite profitable. Figure 5.10 shows the percentage deviations in more detail.

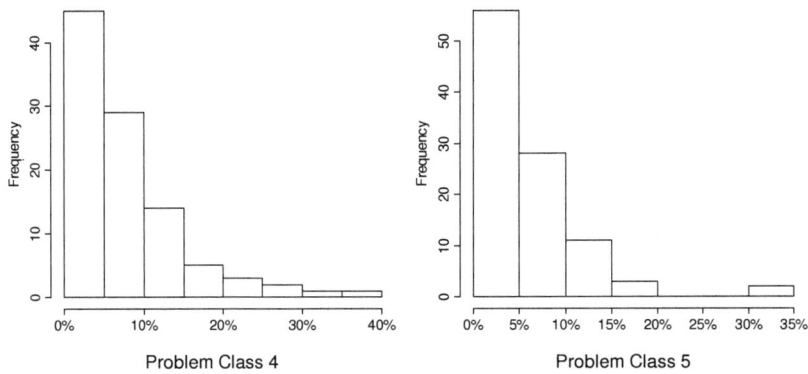

Figure 5.10: Histograms of the percentage deviations $\Delta^{\text{FCFS}-\text{H}}$ of the heuristic policy compared to the FCFS policy

The performance of the heuristic procedure was also investigated for different average lengths of the setup times which can be seen in table 5.10.

problem class →		4	5
problem instances	$(r = 0.9/r = 0.5)$	100/100	100/100
average [%]	$(r = 0.9/r = 0.5)$	3.9/6.1	4.6/8.4
minimum [%]	$(r = 0.9/r = 0.5)$	0.0/0.0	0.0/0.0
maximum [%]	$(r = 0.9/r = 0.5)$	19.2/29.2	32.2/37.8
standard deviation [%]	$(r = 0.9/r = 0.5)$	4.2/5.3	5.0/7.7

Table 5.10: $\Delta^{\text{FCFS}-\text{H}}$ with low $(r = 0.9)$ and high $(r = 0.5)$ setup times

It can be seen that the heuristic procedure performs better with higher setup times than with lower setup times which can be expected because the potential of revenue management correlates with the average length of setup times, see table 5.3. The percentage deviations in table 5.10 show that substantial improvements can be achieved by the heuristic procedure. Figure 5.11 shows the percentage deviations in more detail.

Table 5.11 shows the comparison of the heuristic procedure to a FCFS policy at different traffic intensities. As can be expected, the performance improvements are directly correlated to the traffic intensity. Table 5.11 shows that the performance improvements by the heuristic procedure can be substantial and figure 5.12 shows the percentage deviations in more detail.

problem class →		4	5
problem instances	$(\tilde{\rho} = 1/\tilde{\rho} = 2.5)$	100/100	100/100
average [%]	$(\tilde{\rho} = 1/\tilde{\rho} = 2.5)$	1.8/11.5	2.2/13.1
minimum [%]	$(\tilde{\rho} = 1/\tilde{\rho} = 2.5)$	0.0/0.0	0.0/0.0
maximum [%]	$(\tilde{\rho} = 1/\tilde{\rho} = 2.5)$	18.3/44.5	12.8/48.2
standard deviation [%]	$(\tilde{\rho} = 1/\tilde{\rho} = 2.5)$	2.4/8.3	2.4/9.8

Table 5.11: $\Delta^{\text{FCFS}-\text{H}}$ with different approximate traffic intensities $\tilde{\rho}$

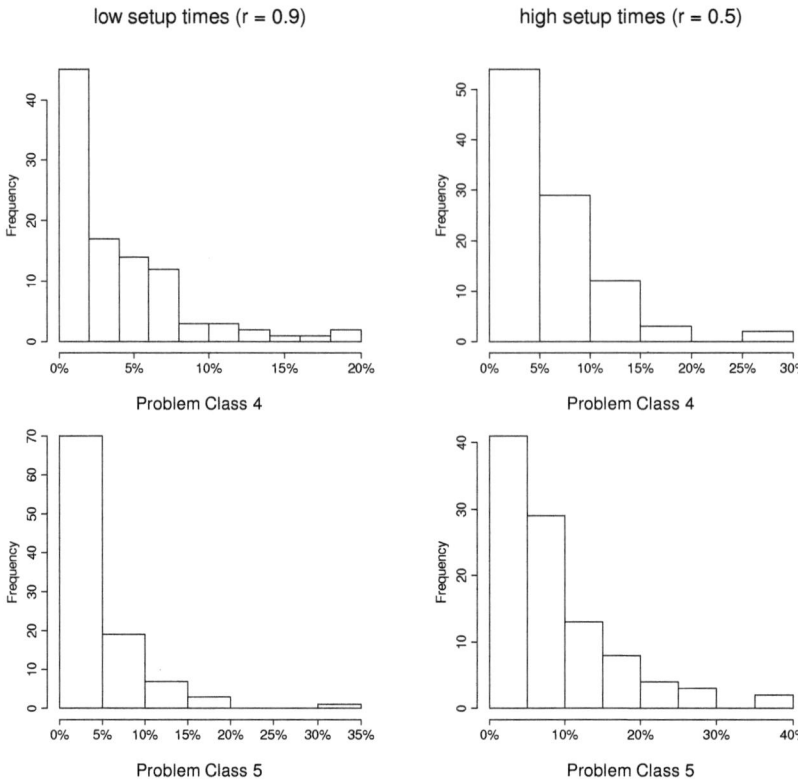

Figure 5.11: Histograms of the percentage deviations $\Delta^{\mathrm{FCFS-H}}$ with low and high setup times

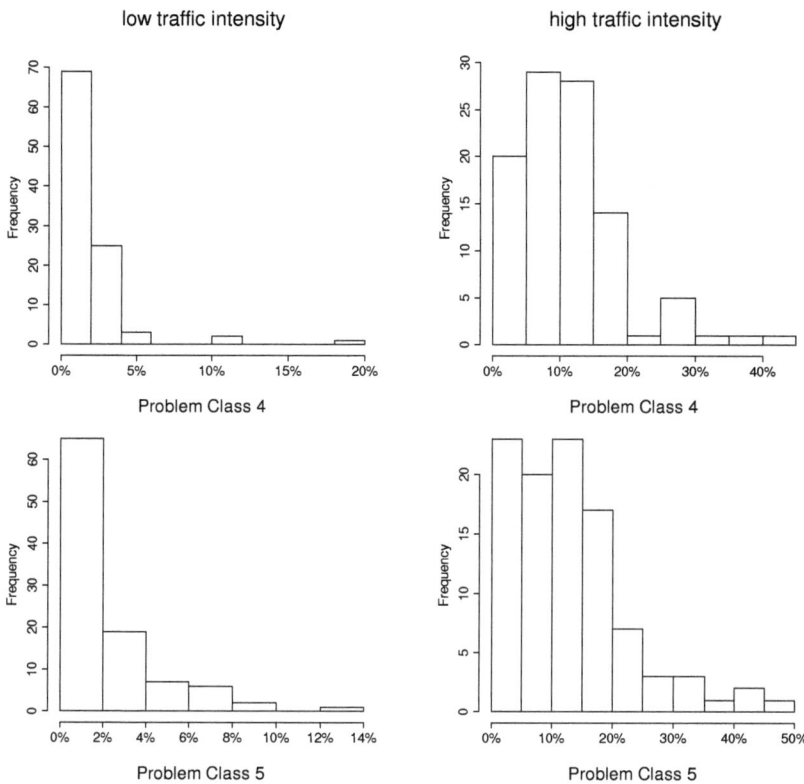

Figure 5.12: Histograms of the percentage deviations $\Delta^{\text{FCFS}-\text{H}}$ at varying traffic intensities

Concluding the numerical tests for this chapter, it was shown that revenue management has a significant advantage over a FCFS policy. The heuristic procedure performed quite well on average, but there were maximum percentage deviations from the optimal procedure up to 16% which suggest that an optimal procedure should be used when available. The heuristic procedure proved suitable to significantly improve the average reward of a FCFS policy for large problem instances, which would make it the method of choice for an implementation for large real-world problem instances.

Chapter 6

Conclusions and Future Research

In this dissertation, the potential benefits of applying revenue management to manufacturing companies were investigated. The general conclusion that can be drawn is that revenue management can have a significant impact on the bottom line of manufacturing companies. The numerical tests showed that by using revenue management, the profitability of a company can be increased significantly, which in turn strengthens the company's position in a global market. In one real-world case, not using revenue management drove a company out of business, see the quote of Donald Burr, former CEO of PeopleExpress in Cross (1997). Another real-world example shows that American Airlines was able to generate US\$1.4 billion in additional revenue over a three-year period in 1988, see Smith, Leimkuhler, and Darrow (1992). While these examples might not be representative for manufacturing companies, they show that revenue management can have a deep impact on a company's business.

The potential of revenue management for manufacturing companies was exemplified in the second chapter, where an empirical study showed that there exists a substantial potential for revenue management in manufacturing industries which has not been fully tapped yet.

In the following chapters, a basic quantitative model for applying revenue management in a manufacturing context was formulated as a Markov decision process and expanded. Chapter 3 started by presenting a basic quantitative model for revenue management and classifying it. After that, six different procedures to evaluate the average reward of a given policy are compared with

© Springer Fachmedien Wiesbaden GmbH, part of Springer Nature 2009
F. Defregger, *Revenue Management for Manufacturing Companies*, Edition KWV,
https://doi.org/10.1007/978-3-658-24037-0_6

regards to their running times. It turned out that evaluating the evaluation equations with a modified Gauss-Seidel method was the fastest procedure for small problem instances while simulation was the only viable method for large problem instances. Chapter 3 continued with a comparison of three standard procedures for solving a Markov decision process and it turned out that the policy iteration method was the fastest method while no solution method could solve the Markov decision process for a large problem instance within a time limit of one hour. Thus, a heuristic solution procedure was presented in order to solve the Markov decision process in a short amount of time resulting in a relatively good average reward per period. Numerical tests concluded this chapter which showed that revenue management has a significant potential compared to a simple FCFS policy and that the heuristic procedure performs reasonably well for a wide array of problem classes.

In chapter 4, the basic model of chapter 3 was expanded by the possibility to store a single product type in an inventory with limited inventory capacity. After an adequate mathematical model was formulated and classified, a heuristic procedure was presented which consists of two parts. First, a suitable maximum inventory level is found which is necessary in order to take into account the inventory holding costs. A suitable trade-off has to be found between the inventory holding costs which might be quite high and the advantages of being able to fulfill more orders with a rising inventory level. In the second part, the heuristic procedure tries to find the right amount of orders which should be rejected in order to reserve enough capacity for more profitable orders. Following the description of the heuristic procedure, it was shown in a number of numerical tests that revenue management can have a significant impact on the average reward per period when compared to a simple FCFS policy which chooses a maximum inventory level of either zero or the maximum inventory capacity, depending on the inventory holding costs. It was also shown that when inventory holding costs are high, the impact of using revenue management becomes rather small because the optimal inventory level is zero and thus the traffic intensity is effectively reduced because less orders can be accepted.

Chapter 5 expanded the basic model of chapter 3 by allowing for sequence-dependent setup times and costs for multiple order classes. After an appropriate model had been formulated and classified, a heuristic procedure was introduced which uses a similar technique to the first part of the heuristic procedure in chapter 4. In the course of the numerical tests it turned out that it was more difficult to control the traffic intensity than in the previous chapters because setup times have an impact on resource utilization as well. As a remedy, a procedure to create problem instances was introduced which was able to control the approximate traffic intensity and the ratio of setup times to usage times of each order class. In the course of the numerical tests it turned out an ϵ-optimal policy obtained by value iteration outperforms a simple FCFS policy significantly. The performance of the heuristic procedure was also compared to the ϵ-optimal policy for small problem instances and to a FCFS policy for large problem instances. It turned out that the heuristic procedure performs well and is able to produce significant improvements for large problem instances.

One further question is how the mathematical models could be implemented in a real-world revenue management system and how the necessary input data for the mathematical models could be obtained. After a segmentation of customer orders into order classes has been obtained, the arrival probabilities of the different order classes would have to be estimated. This could be achieved by simply counting arriving orders over a longer investigation period Π to obtain an arrival rate for each order class. As the time-discrete Markov decision models imply geometrically distributed interarrival times of the orders, the arrival probability of the orders could be calculated from the mean of the geometric distribution of the interarrival times. This mean could be calculated for the investigation period Π by dividing by the number of orders which have arrived during this period. For example, if 5 orders of a certain order class n arrived over an investigation period of $\Pi = 10$ days, the geometric mean of the interarrival times would be 2 days. Thus, the arrival probability would be calculated by $p_n = 1/2 = 0.5$. The profit margins m_n could be obtained from the accounting department and the usage times u_n from the production management department while the lead times l_n could be obtained from the customers.

One specific question with regards to an implementation of the mathematical models would also be the length of the discrete time periods used in the mathematical decision models. A finer time discretization would be a more accurate representation of reality, but the mathematical models would become more difficult to solve because of a larger state space. Thus, one would have to find a time-discretization that would it still make possible not to overuse the given memory capacity of the computer that solves the mathematical decision problem.

Another interesting aspect of the mathematical models is the link between capacity control and dynamic pricing. While the mathematical models solve a capacity control problem, it turns out that the stochastic process resulting from an optimal policy reflects the solution of a dynamic pricing problem. This is shown in a fictitious example in figure 6.1.

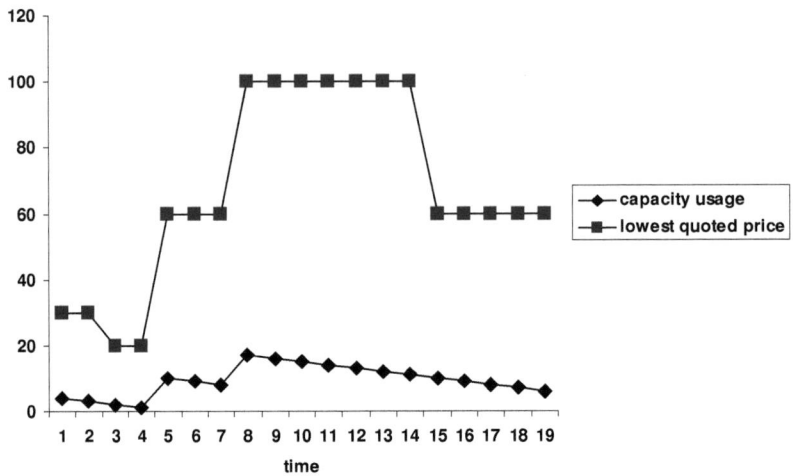

Figure 6.1: Stochastic process which results in dynamic pricing

Figure 6.1 shows that the lowest quoted price for customers varies with the current capacity usage of the resource. In period 2, the capacity usage sinks below a level where an additional order class is accepted. In period 5, an incoming order has been accepted and the capacity usage rises. This causes some order classes to be closed which results in an increase in the lowest price quoted to customers. In period 8, another order is accepted and the capacity usage rises further, then no more order is accepted and the capacity usage decreases by one unit in every period. This simple example shows that the capacity control models in this dissertation can also be used to implement dynamic pricing policies.

With regards to further research opportunities, all mathematical models presented in this dissertation did not allow for any scheduling of orders that have already been accepted. Implementing an opportunity of making orders independent of the order in which they were received at the order acceptance department would make all mathematical models intractable because of an explosion of the state space. Every state would have to use an additional state variable for every order which was already accepted which would lead to an explosion of the state space. Allowing for a rescheduling of orders would considerably increase the average reward per period that can be obtained, but a solution to this problem seems very difficult, but perhaps not impossible.

Summing up, this dissertation has showed that revenue management is already used by a significant fraction of companies in the paper, steel and aluminium industries. The quantitative decision models show that a great potential for applying revenue management in the manufacturing industries exists at least in theory. Implementing these models into the wider frame of a complete revenue management system might be difficult, but the numerical results show that an implementation effort could well be worthwhile. Only time will tell if real decision systems for revenue management based on quantitative decision models will start to take hold on a larger scale in the manufacturing industries.

Bibliography

Agresti, A. (2002). *Categorical Data Analysis* (2nd ed.). Hoboken, New Jersey: Wiley.

Baker, T. and N. N. Murthy (2005). Viability of auction-based revenue management in sequential markets. *Decision Sciences 36*(2), 259–286.

Balachandran, K. R. and M. E. Schaefer (1981). Optimal acceptance of job orders. *International Journal of Production Research 19*(2), 195–200.

Balakrishnan, N., J. W. Patterson, and S. V. Sridharan (1996). Rationing capacity between two product classes. *Decision Sciences 27*(2), 185–214.

Balakrishnan, N., J. W. Patterson, and V. Sridharan (1999). Robustness of capacity rationing policies. *European Journal of Operational Research 115*, 328–338.

Barut, M. and V. Sridharan (2005). Revenue management in order-driven production systems. *Decision Sciences 36*(2), 287–316.

Burden, R. L. and J. D. Faires (1997). *Numerical Analysis* (6th ed.). Pacific Grove, California: Brooks/Cole.

Caldentey, R. (2001). *Analyzing the Make-to-Stock Queue in the Supply Chain and eBusiness Settings*. Ph. D. thesis, Massachusetts Institute of Technology, Cambridge, Massachusetts.

Carr, S. and I. Duenyas (2000). Optimal admission control and sequencing in a make-to-stock/make-to-order production system. *Operations Research 48*(5), 709–720.

Chan, L. M. A., Z. J. Shen, D. Simchi-Levi, and J. L. Swann (2004). Coordination of pricing and inventory decisions: A survey and classification. In D. Simchi-Levi, S. D. Wu, and Z.-J. Shen (Eds.), *Handbook of Quantitative Supply Chain Analysis*, Berlin. Springer.

© Springer Fachmedien Wiesbaden GmbH, part of Springer Nature 2009
F. Defregger, *Revenue Management for Manufacturing Companies*, Edition KWV,
https://doi.org/10.1007/978-3-658-24037-0

Chan, L. M. A., D. Simchi-Levi, and J. L. Swann (2003). Dynamic pricing strategies for manufacturing with stochastic demand and discretionary sales. Working paper.

Chen, H. and M. Z. Frank (2001). State dependent pricing with a queue. *IIE Transactions 33*, 847–860.

Conover, W. J. (1999). *Practical Nonparametric Statistics* (3rd ed.). New York: Wiley.

Cross, R. G. (1997). *Revenue Management: Hardcore Tactics for Market Domination.* New York: Broadway Books.

D'Agostino, R. B. and M. A. Stephens (1986). *Goodness-Of-Fit-Techniques.* New York: Dekker.

Defregger, F. and H. Kuhn (2004). Revenue management in manufacturing. In Ahr, D. et al. (Ed.), *Operations Research Proceedings 2003*, Berlin, pp. 17–22. Springer.

Defregger, F. and H. Kuhn (2007). Revenue management for a make-to-order company with limited inventory capacity. *OR Spectrum 29*(1), 137–156.

Duenyas, I. (1995). Single facility due date setting with multiple customer classes. *Management Science 41*(4), 608–619.

Duenyas, I. and W. J. Hopp (1995). Quoting customer lead times. *Management Science 41*(1), 43–57.

Easton, F. F. and D. R. Moodie (1999). Pricing and lead time decisions for make-to-order firms with contingent orders. *European Journal of Operational Research 116*, 305–318.

Elimam, A. A. and B. M. Dodin (2001). Incentives and yield management in improving productivity of manufacturing facilities. *IIE Transactions 33*, 449–462.

Gallego, G. and G. van Ryzin (1997). A multi-product dynamic pricing problem and its applications to network yield management. *Operations Research 45*, 24–41.

Gallien, J. and L. M. Wein (2005). A smart market for industrial procurement with capacity constraints. *Management Science 51*(1), 76–91.

Harris, F. H. d. and J. P. Pinder (1995). A revenue management approach to demand management and order booking in assemble-to-order manufacturing. *Journal of Operations Management 13*(4), 299–309.

Kapuscinski, R. and S. Tayur (2000). Dynamic capacity reservation in a make-to-order environment. Working paper.

Keilson, J. (1970). A simple algorithm for contract acceptance. *Opsearch 7*, 157–166.

Keskinocak, P., R. Ravi, and S. Tayur (2001). Scheduling and reliable lead-time quotation for orders with availability intervals and lead-time sensitive revenues. *Management Science 47*(2), 264–279.

Kimes, S. E. (1989). Yield management: A tool for capacity-constrained service firms. *Journal of Operations Management 8*(4), 348–363.

Kniker, T. S. and M. H. Burman (2001). Applications of revenue management to manufacturing. In *Third Aegean International Conference on Design and Analysis of Manufacturing Systems, May 19–22, 2001, Tinos Island, Greece*, Thessaloniki, Greece, pp. 299–308. Editions Ziti.

Kuhn, H. and F. Defregger (2005). Revenue Management in der Sachleistungswirtschaft. Eine empirische Untersuchung am Beispiel der Papier-, Stahl- und Aluminiumindustrie. Discussion Papers of the Faculty of Business Administration and Economics, Ingolstadt, Nr. 171. Catholic University Eichstätt-Ingolstadt.

Kulkarni, V. G. (1999). *Modeling, Analysis, Design, and Control of Stochastic Systems*. New York: Springer.

Law, A. M. and W. D. Kelton (2000). *Simulation Modeling and Analysis* (3rd ed.). Boston: McGraw-Hill.

L'Ecuyer, P. (1999). Good parameters and implementations for combined multiple recursive random number generators. *Operations Research 47*(1), 159–164.

L'Ecuyer, P. (2001). Software for uniform random number generation: Distringuishing the good and the bad. In B. A. Peters, J. S. Smith, D. J. Medeiros, and M. W. Rohrer (Eds.), *Proceedings of the 2001 Winter Simulation Conference*, pp. 95–105.

Lippman, S. A. (1975). Applying a new device in the optimization of exponential queuing systems. *Operations Research 23*(4), 687–710.

Lippman, S. A. and S. M. Ross (1971). The streetwalker's dilemma: A job shop model. *SIAM Journal on Applied Mathematics 20*(3), 336–342.

Low, D. W. (1974). Optimal dynamic pricing policies for an M/M/s queue. *Operations Research 22*(3), 545–561.

Matsui, M. (1982). Job-shop model: a M/(G,G)/1(N) production system with order selection. *International Journal of Production Research 20*(2), 201–210.

Matsui, M. (1985). Optimal order-selection policies for a job shop production system. *International Journal of Production Research 23*(1), 21–31.

McGill, J. I. and G. J. van Ryzin (1999). Revenue management: Research overview and prospects. *Transportation Science 33*(2), 233–256.

Miller, B. L. (1969). A queueing reward system with several customer classes. *Management Science 16*(3), 234–245.

Missbauer, H. (2003). Optimal lower bounds on the contribution margin in the case of stochastic order arrival. *OR Spectrum 25*(4), 497–519.

Patterson, J. W., N. Balakrishnan, and Sridharan (1997). An experimental comparison of capacity rationing models. *International Journal of Production Research 35*(6), 1639–1649.

Puterman, M. L. (1994). *Markov Decision Processes*. New York: Wiley.

R Development Core Team (2007). *R: A Language and Environment for Statistical Computing*. Vienna: R Foundation for Statistical Computing. http://www.R-project.org.

Seneta, E. (1993). Probability inequalities and Dunnett's test. In F. M. Hoppe (Ed.), *Multiple Comparisons, Selection and Application in Biometry*, New York, pp. 29–45. Dekker.

Smith, B. C., J. F. Leimkuhler, and R. M. Darrow (1992). Yield management at american airlines. *Interfaces 22*, 8–31.

Stewart, W. J. (1994). *Introduction to the Numerical Solution of Markov Chains*. Princeton, New Jersey: Princeton University Press.

Swann, J. L. (1999). Flexible pricing policies: Introduction and a survey of implementation in various industries. Technical Report CR-99/04/ESL, Northwestern University, Evanston, Illinois.

Swann, J. L. (2001). *Dynamic Pricing Models to Improve Supply Chain Performance*. Ph. D. thesis, Northwestern University, Evanston, Illinois.

Talluri, K. T. and G. J. van Ryzin (2004). *The Theory and Practice of Revenue Management*. Boston: Kluwer.

Thode, H. C. (2002). *Testing for Normality*. New York: Dekker.

Tijms, H. C. (1994). *Stochastic models: an algorithmic approach*. Chichester, United Kingdom: Wiley.

Watanapa, B. and A. Techanitisawad (2005). Simultaneous price and due date settings for multiple customer classes. *European Journal of Operational Research 166*, 351–368.

Wendell, J. P. and J. Schmee (2001). Likelihood confidence intervals for proportions in finite populations. *The American Statistician 55*(1), 55–61.

Wong, J.-T., F. S. Koppelman, and M. S. Daskin (1993). Flexible assignment approach to itinerary seat allocation. *Transportation Research 27B*, 33–48.

Ziya, S., A. Hayriye, and R. D. Foley (2006). Optimal prices for finite capacity queueing systems. *Operations Research Letters 34*, 214–218.